Arch Linux Handbook

Retrieved August 27, 2009

Copyright © 2009 by Dusty Phillips

Retrieved August 27, 2009 from
http://wiki.archlinux.org/index.php/Beginners_Guide

Permission is granted to copy, distribute and/or modify this
document under the terms of the GNU Free Documentation
License, Version 1.2 or any later version published by the Free
Software Foundation; with no Invariant Sections, no Front-Cover
Texts, and no Back-Cover Texts. A copy of the license is
included in the section entitled "GNU Free Documentation
License".

For information on this booklet, please contact Dusty Phillips at
dusty@archlinux.ca

Cover and Book Design by Dusty Phillips.

Printed in the United States by Amazon CreateSpace.
Designed in Canada.

EAN-13: 9781448699605
ISBN-10: 1448699606

Table of Contents

Table of Contents..1
Preface..5
Part I: Install the Base System........................9
    Step 1: Obtain the latest Installation media 9
    Step 2: Boot Arch Linux Installer.........................11
    Step 3: Start the Installation.............................12
    A: Select an installation source........................12
    B: Set Clock..15
    C: Prepare Hard Drive..................................15
    D: Select Packages.......................................24
    E: Install Packages......................................25
    F: Configure the System...............................25
    G: Install Bootloader....................................42
    H: Reboot...44
Part II: Configure&Update the New Arch Linux base
system...45
    Step 1: Configuring the network (if necessary)........45
    Step 2: Update, Sync and Upgrade the system with
    pacman...51
    Step 3: Update System....................................62
    Step 4: Add a user and setup groups....................63
    Step 5: Install and setup Sudo (Optional)...............65
Part III: Install X and configure ALSA..............67
    Step 1: Configure sound with alsamixer................67
    Step 2: Install X...70
    Step 3: Configure X.......................................77
    Simple baseline X test(if necessary)...................84
Part IV: Installing and configuring a Desktop
Environment 89
    Step 1: Install Fonts......................................90
    Step 2: ~/.xinitrc (again).................................90

Arch Linux Handbook

Step 3: Install a Desktop Environment.....................91
Useful Applications..105
    Web browser..105
    Office..106
    Video Player...106
    Audio Player...109
    Codecs and other multimedia content types (i686
    only) 111
    CD and DVD Burning...112
    Networking..113
    TV-Cards...114
    Digital Cameras..115
    USB Memory Sticks / Hard Disks..........................115
An Introduction to ABS..117
An Introduction to The AUR..121
    Install an AUR Helper...123
File and directory explanation......................................125
Arch Boot Process..135
    Boot Script Overview...136
    agetty and login..139
Maintaining the system..141
    su...141
    Pacman..142
Tweaks/Finishing touches..149
    HAL...149
    Backgrounding DAEMONS on startup...................149
    Turn off Control Echo in Bash...............................150
    Beautifying Fonts for LCD's...................................150
    Adjusting Mouse for scroll wheel..........................150
    Get All Mouse Buttons Working.............................150
    Configuring Touchpad for Laptops.........................150
    Adjusting Keyboard Layout....................................150
    Additional tweaks for laptops.................................151
    Configuring CPU frequency scaling.......................151

2

Table of Contents

Pm-Utils...152
Laptop-Mode...152
Add additional repositories....................................153
GNU Free Documentation License............................155
GNU Free Documentation License.......................155
How to use this License for your documents.........164

Preface

Everything you ever wanted to know about Arch, but were afraid to ask

Welcome. This self-contained document will guide you through the process of installing and configuring Arch Linux; a simple, agile and lightweight GNU/Linux distribution, UNIX-like operating system. Arch Linux requires a certain level of intimate knowledge of its configuration and of UNIX-like system methodology and for this reason, extra explanatory information is included. This guide is aimed at new Arch users, but strives to serve as a strong reference and informative base for all.

Arch Linux distribution highlights:

- **Simple**, UNIX-like design and philosophy
- Independently Developed Community distro built from scratch and targeted at competent GNU/Linux users
- All packages compiled for **i686/x86-64**
- Highly customizable system assembled by the user from the ground up
- **BSD-style init** scripts, featuring one centralized configuration file
- **mkinitcpio**: a simple and dynamic initramfs creator
- **Rolling Release** model
- **Pacman** package manager is fast, written in **C**, lightweight and agile, with a very modest memory footprint
- **ABS**: The Arch Build System, a ports-like package building system makes it simple to create your own easily installable Arch packages from source, to use and/or share with the community on the AUR
- **AUR**: The Arch User Repository, offering many thousands of build scripts for Arch user-provided software packages

Arch Linux Handbook

DON'T PANIC !

The Arch Linux system is assembled by the *user*, from the shell, using basic command line tools. This is **The Arch Way.** Unlike the more rigid structures of other distributions and installers, there are no default environments nor configurations chosen for you. From the command line, *you* will add packages from the Arch repositories using the pacman tool via your internet connection and manually configure your installation by editing text files until your system is customized to your requirements. You will also manually add non-root user(s) and manage groups and permissions. This method allows for maximum flexibility, choice, and system resource control *from the base up.*

Arch Linux is aimed at competent GNU/Linux users who desire minimal 'code separation' from their machine.

License

Arch Linux, pacman, documentation, and scripts are copyright ©2002-2007 by Judd Vinet, ©2007-2009 by Aaron Griffin and are licensed under the GNU General Public License Version 2.

The Arch Way

The design principles behind Arch are aimed at keeping it simple.

'Simple', in this context, shall mean 'without unnecessary additions, modifications, or complications'.. In. short; an elegant, minimalist approach.

Some thoughts to keep in mind:

- " 'Simple' is defined from a technical standpoint, not a *usability standpoint. It is better to be technically elegant with a higher learning curve, than to be easy to use and technically [inferior]." -Aaron Griffin*
- *Entia non sunt multiplicanda praeter necessitatem* or "Entities should not be multiplied unnecessarily." -Occam's razor. The term *razor* refers to the act of shaving away unnecessary complications to arrive at the simplest explanation, method or theory.

Preface

- *"The extraordinary part of [my method] lies in its simplicity..The height of cultivation always runs to simplicity."* - Bruce Lee

About This Guide

The Arch wiki is an excellent resource and should be consulted for issues first; IRC (freenode #archlinux), and the forums are also available if the answer cannot be found.

> **Note**: Following this guide closely is essential in order to successfully install a properly configured Arch Linux system, so please read it thoroughly. It is strongly recommended you read each section completely before carrying out the tasks contained.

Since GNU/Linux Distributions are fundamentally 'modular' by design, the guide is logically divided into 4 main components of a desktop UNIX-like operating system:

Part I: Installing the Base system

Part II: Configure&Update the New Arch Linux base system

Part III: Installing X and configuring ALSA

Part IV: Installing a Desktop Environment

Welcome to Arch! Enjoy the installation; take your time and have fun!

Now, let's get started....

Part I: Install the Base System

Step 1: Obtain the latest Installation media

You can obtain Arch's official installation media from http://archlinux.org/download/. The latest version is 2009.08

- Both the Core installer and the FTP/HTTP-downloads provide only the necessary packages to create an **Arch Linux base system**. *Note that the Base System does not include a GUI. It is mainly comprised of the GNU toolchain (compiler, assembler, linker, libraries, shell, and a few useful utilities), the Linux kernel, and a few extra libraries and modules.*
- The isolinux images are provided for people who experience trouble using the grub version. There are no other differences.
- The Arch64 FAQ (http://wiki.archlinux.org/index.php/Arch64_FAQ) can help you chose between the 32- and 64-bit versions.

CD installer

Burn the .iso to a CD with your preferred burner, and continue with Step 2: Boot Arch Linux Installer

Note: Optical drives as well as CD media quality vary greatly, but generally, using a slow burn speed is recommended for reliable burns; Some users recommend speeds as low as 4x or 2x. If you are experiencing unexpected behavior from the CD, try burning at the minimum speed supported by your system.

Arch Linux Handbook

USB stick

> Warning: This will irrevocably destroy all data on your USB stick.

UNIX Method:

Insert an empty or expendable USB stick, determine its path, and dump the .img to the USB stick with the **/bin/dd** program:

```
dd if=archlinux-2009.08-[core_or_ftp]-i686.img
of=/dev/sdx
```

where *if=* is the path to the img file and *of=* is your USB device. Make sure to use /dev/sdx and not /dev/sdx1.

Check md5sum (optional):

Make a note of the number of records (blocks) read in and written out, then perform the following check:

```
dd if=/dev/sdx count=number_of_records status=noxfer |
md5sum
```

The md5sum returned should match the md5sum of the downloaded archlinux image file; they both should match the md5sum of the image as listed in the md5sums file in the mirror distribution site.

Windows Method:

Download Disk Imager from https://launchpad.net/win32-image-writer/+download. Insert flash media. Start the Disk Imager and select the image file. Select the Drive letter associated with the flash drive. Click "write".

Continue with Step 2: Boot Arch Linux Installer

Part I: Install the Base System

Step 2: Boot Arch Linux Installer

Insert the CD or USB stick and boot from it. You may have to change the boot order in your computer BIOS or press a key (usually DEL, F1, F2, F11 or F12) during the BIOS POST phase.

Memory requirements:

- CORE : 160 MB RAM x86_64/i686 (all packages selected, with swap partition)
- FTP : 160 MB RAM x86_64/i686 (all packages selected, with swap partition)

Choose Boot Archlive or Boot Archlive [legacy IDE] if you have trouble with libata/PATA.

To change boot options press **e** for editing the boot lines. Many users may wish to change the resolution of the framebuffer, for more readable console output. Append:

```
vga=773
```

to the kernel line, followed by <ENTER>, for a 1024x768 framebuffer.

Hit **b** to boot.

The system will now boot and present a login prompt. Login as 'root' without quotes.

If your system has errors trying to boot from the live CD or there are other **hardware** errors, refer to the Installation Troubleshooting wiki page.

Changing the keymap

If you have a non-US keyboard layout you can interactively choose your keymap/console font with the command:

11

Arch Linux Handbook

```
# km
```

or use the loadkeys command:

```
# loadkeys layout
```

(replace *layout* with your keyboard layout such as "fr" or "be-latin1")

Documentation

The official install guide is available on the live system. The official guide covers installation and configuration of the base system only. Change to vc/2 (virtual console #2) with <ALT>+F2 and invoke /usr/bin/less:

```
# less /arch/docs/official_installation_guide_en
```

less will allow you to page through the document. Change back to vc/1 with <ALT>+F1.

Change back to vc/2 if you need to reference the Official Guide at any time.

Step 3: Start the Installation

As root, run the installer script from vc/1:

```
# /arch/setup
```

A: Select an installation source

After a welcome screen, you will be prompted for an installation source. Choose the appropriate source for the installer you are using.

Part I: Install the Base System

- If you chose the CORE installer, continue below with C: Prepare Hard Drive.
- FTP/HTTP only: You shall be prompted to load ethernet drivers manually, if desired. Udev is quite effective at loading the required modules, so you may assume it has already done so. You may verify this by invoking ifconfig -a from vc/3. (Select OK to continue.)

Configure Network (FTP/HTTP)

Available Interfaces will be presented. If an interface and HWaddr (**HardW**are **addr**ess) is listed, then your module has already been loaded. If your interface is not listed, you may probe it from the installer, or manually do so from another virtual console.

The following screen will prompt you to *Select the interface, Probe,* or *Cancel*. Choose the appropriate interface and continue.

The installer will then ask if you wish to use DHCP. Choosing Yes will run **dhcpcd** to discover an available gateway and request an IP address; Choosing No will prompt you for your static IP, netmask, broadcast, gateway DNS IP, HTTP proxy, and FTP proxy. Lastly, you will be presented with an overview to ensure your entries are correct.

Wireless Quickstart For the Live Environment (If you need wireless connectivity during the installation process)

The wireless drivers and utilities are now available to you in the live environment of the installation media. A good knowledge of your wireless hardware will be of key importance to successful configuration. Note that the following quickstart procedure will initialize your wireless hardware for use *in the live environment*.

The basic procedure will be:

- Switch to a free virtual console, e.g.: <ALT>+F3
- Ensure udev has loaded the driver, and that the driver has created a usable wireless kernel interface with `/usr/sbin/iwconfig`:

13

Arch Linux Handbook

```
# iwconfig
```

(Output should show an available wireless interface)

- Bring the interface up with /sbin/ifconfig <interface> up.

An example, using an atheros card and madwifi driver:

```
# ifconfig ath0 up
```

(Remember, your interface may be named something else, depending on your module (driver) and chipset: wlan0, eth1, etc.)

- Specify the id of the wireless network with iwconfig <interface> essid "<youressid>" key <yourwepkey> (give the essid (the 'network name') of the network in quotes).
- An example using WEP:

```
# iwconfig ath0 essid "linksys" key 0241baf34c
```

- An example using an unsecured network:

```
# iwconfig ath0 essid "linksys"
```

- Request and acquire an IP address with /sbin/dhcpcd <interface> . e.g.:

```
# dhcpcd ath0
```

- Ensure you can route using /bin/ping:

```
# ping -c 3 www.google.com
```

Done.

14

Part I: Install the Base System

Note: In addition to the wireless module, some wireless chipsets, like ipw2100 and ipw2200, require corresponding firmware installation. The firmware packages must be explicitly installed to your actual system to provide wireless functionality after you reboot into your installed system. (Due to the firmware installation requirement, these chipsets may not work in the live environment.) Package selection and installation is covered below. Ensure installation of both your wireless module and firmware during the package selection step! See Wireless Setup if you are unsure about the requirement of corresponding firmware installation for your particular chipset. This is a very common error.

After the initial Arch installation is complete, you may wish to refer to Wireless Setup to ensure a permanent configuration solution for your installed system.

Return to vc/1 with <ALT>+F1. Continue with C: Prepare Hard Drive

B: Set Clock

- UTC - Choose UTC if running only UNIX-like operating system(s).

- localtime - Choose local if multi-booting with a Microsoft Windows OS.

C: Prepare Hard Drive

Warning: Partitioning hard drives can destroy data. You are strongly cautioned and advised to backup your critical data if applicable.

Verify current disk identities and layout by invoking /sbin/fdisk with the -l (lower-case L) switch.

Open another virtual console (<ALT>+F3) and enter:

15

Arch Linux Handbook

```
# fdisk -l
```

Take note of the disk(s)/partition(s) to utilize for the Arch installation.

Switch back to the installation script with <ALT>+F1

Select the first menu entry "Prepare Hard Drive".

- Option 1: Auto Prepare

Auto-Prepare divides the disk into the following configuration:

- ext2 /boot partition, default size 32MB. *You will be prompted to modify the size to your requirement.*
- swap partition, default size 256MB. *You will be prompted to modify the size to your requirement.*
- A Separate / and /home partition, (sizes can also be specified). Available filesystems include ext2, ext3, ext4, reiserfs, xfs and jfs, but note that *both / and /home shall share the same fs type* if choosing the Auto Prepare option.

Be warned that Auto-prepare will completely erase the chosen hard drive. Read the warning presented by the installer very carefully, and make sure the correct device is about to be partitioned.

- Option 2: **(Recommended)** Partition Hard Drives (with cfdisk)

This option will allow for the most robust and customized partitioning solution for your personal needs.

*At this point, more advanced GNU/Linux users who are familiar and comfortable with manually partitioning may wish to skip down to **D: Select Packages** below.*

Note: If you are installing to a USB flash key, see "Installing Arch Linux on a USB key".

Part I: Install the Base System

Partition Hard Drives

Partition Info

Partitioning a hard disk drive defines specific areas (the partitions) within the disk, that will each appear and behave as a separate disk and upon which a filesystem may be created (formatted).

- There are 3 types of disk partitions:

1. Primary
2. Extended
3. Logical

Primary partitions can be bootable, and are limited to 4 partitions per disk or raid volume. If a partitioning scheme requires more than 4 partitions, an **extended** partition which will contain **logical** partitions will be required.

Extended partitions are not usable by themselves; they are merely a "container" for logical partitions. If required, a hard disk shall contain only one extended partition; which shall then be sub-divided into logical partitions.

When partitioning a disk, one can observe this numbering scheme by creating primary partitions sda1-3 followed by creating an extended partition, sda4, and subsequently creating logical partition(s) within the extended partition; sda5, sda6, and so on.

Swap Partition

A swap partition is a place on the drive where virtual ram resides, allowing the kernel to easily use disk storage for data that does not fit into physical RAM.

Historically, the general rule for swap partition size was 2x the amount of physical RAM. Over time, as computers have gained ever larger memory capacities, this rule has become increasingly deprecated. Generally, on machines with up to 512MB RAM, the 2x rule is usually quite sufficient. On machines with 1GB RAM, generally a 1x rule is adequate. If the installation machine provides gratuitous amounts of RAM (more than 1024 MB) it may be

Arch Linux Handbook

possible to completely forget a swap partition altogether, though this is not recommended. A 1 GB swap partition will be used in this example.

> **Note**: If using suspend-to-disk, (hibernate) a swap partition at least **equal** in size to the amount of physical RAM is required. Some Arch users even recommend oversizing it beyond the amount of physical RAM by 10-15%, to allow for possible bad sectors.

Partition Scheme

A disk partitioning scheme is a very personalized preference. Each user's choices will be unique to their own computing habits and requirements.

Filesystem candidates for separate partitions include:

/ (root) *The root filesystem is the primary filesystem from which all other filesystems stem; the top of the hierarchy. All files and directories appear under the root directory "/", even if they are stored on different physical devices. The contents of the root filesystem must be adequate to boot, restore, recover, and/or repair the system.*

/boot *This directory contains the kernel and ramdisk images as well as the bootloader configuration file, and bootloader stages. /boot also stores data that is used before the kernel begins executing userspace programs. This may include saved master boot sectors and sector map files.*

/home *User data and user specific configuration files for applications are stored in each user's home directory in a file that starts with the '.' character (a "dot file").*

/usr *While root is the primary filesystem, /usr is the secondary hierarchy, for user data, containing the majority of (multi-)user utilities and applications. /usr is shareable, read-only data. This means that /usr shall be shareable between various hosts and must not be written to, except in the case of system update/upgrade. Any*

18

Part I: Install the Base System

information that is host-specific or varies with time is stored elsewhere.

/tmp *directory for programs that require temporary files*

/var *contains variable data; spool directories and files, administrative and logging data, pacman's cache, the ABS tree, etc.*

> **Note**: Besides /boot, directories essential for booting are: '/bin', '/dev', '/etc', '/lib', '/proc' and '/sbin'. Therefore, they must not reside on a separate partition from /.

There are several advantages for using discrete filesystems, rather than combining all into one partition:

- Security: Each filesystem may be configured in /etc/fstab as 'nosuid', 'nodev', 'noexec', 'readonly', etc.
- Stability: A user, or malfunctioning program can completely fill a filesystem with garbage if they have write permissions for it. Critical programs, which reside on a different filesystem remain unaffected.
- Speed: A filesystem which gets written to frequently may become somewhat fragmented. (An effective method of avoiding fragmentation is to ensure that each filesystem is never in danger of filling up completely.) Separate filesystems remain unaffected, and each can be defragmented separately as well.
- Integrity: If one filesystem becomes corrupted, separate filesystems remain unaffected.
- Versatility: Sharing data across several systems becomes more expedient when independent filesystems are used. Separate filesystem types may also be chosen based upon the nature of data and usage.

In this example, we shall use separate partitions for /, /var, /home, and a swap partition.

19

Arch Linux Handbook

> **Note**: /var contains many small files. This should be taken into consideration when choosing a filesystem type for it, (if creating its own separate partition).

How big should my partitions be?

This question is best answered based upon individual needs. You may wish to simply create **one partition for root and one partition for swap or only one root partition without swap** or refer to the following examples and consider these guidelines to provide a frame of reference:

- The root filesystem (/) in the example will contain the /usr directory, which can become moderately large, depending upon how much software is installed. 15-20 GB should be sufficient for most users.

- The /var filesystem will contain, among other data, the ABS tree and the pacman cache. Keeping cached packages is useful and versatile; it provides the ability to downgrade packages if needed. /var tends to grow in size; the pacman cache can grow large over long periods of time, but can be safely cleared if needed. Another advantage of having a dedicated /var partition is if you're using an SSD. Locate your /var on an HDD and keep the / and /home partitions on your SSD to avoid needless read/writes to the SSD. 6-8 Gigs on a desktop system should therefore be sufficient for /var. Servers tend to have extremely large /var filesystems.

- The /home filesystem is typically where user data, downloads, and multimedia reside. On a desktop system, /home is typically the largest filesystem on the drive by a large margin. Remember that if you chose to reinstall Arch, all the data on your /home partition will be untouched (so long as you have a separate /home partition).

Part I: Install the Base System

- An extra 25% of space added to each filesystem will provide a cushion for unforeseen occurrence, expansion, and serve as a preventive against fragmentation.

From the guidelines above, the example system shall contain a ~15GB root (/) partition, ~7GB /var, 1GB swap, and a /home containing the remaining disk space.

Create Partition:cfdisk

Start by creating the primary partition that will contain the **root**, (/) filesystem.

Choose **New** -> Primary and enter the desired size for root (/). Put the partition at the beginning of the disk.

Also choose the **Type** by designating it as '83 Linux'. The created / partition shall appear as sda1 in our example.

Now create a primary partition for /var, designating it as **Type** 83 Linux. The created /var partition shall appear as sda2

Next, create a partition for swap. Select an appropriate size and specify the **Type** as 82 (Linux swap / Solaris). The created swap partition shall appear as sda3.

Lastly, create a partition for your /home directory. Choose another primary partition and set the desired size.

Likewise, select the **Type** as 83 Linux. The created /home partition shall appear as sda4.

Example:

```
Name    Flags     Part Type     FS Type [Label] Size (MB)
--------------------------------------------------------
sda1              Primary       Linux           15440 #root
sda2              Primary       Linux            6256 #/var
sda3              Primary       Linux swap       1024 #swap
sda4              Primary       Linux          140480 #/home
```

Choose **W**rite and type **'yes'**. Beware that this operation may destroy data on your disk. Choose **Q**uit to leave the partitioner.

21

Arch Linux Handbook

Choose Done to leave this menu and continue with "Set Filesystem Mountpoints".

> **Note**: Since the latest developments of the Linux kernel which include the libata and PATA modules, all IDE, SATA and SCSI drives have adopted the sdx naming scheme. This is perfectly normal and should not be a concern.

Set Filesystem Mountpoints

First you will be asked for your swap partition. Choose the appropriate partition (sda3 in this example). You will be asked if you want to create a swap filesystem; select yes. Next, choose where to mount the / (root) directory (sda1 in the example). At this time, you will be asked to specify the filesystem type.

Filesystem Types

Again, a filesystem type is a very subjective matter which comes down to personal preference. Each has its own advantages, disadvantages, and unique idiosyncrasies. Here is a very brief overview of supported filesystems:

1. **ext2** *Second Extended Filesystem*- Old, reliable GNU/Linux filesystem. Very stable, but *without journaling support*. May be inconvenient for root (/) and /home, due to very long fsck's. *An ext2 filesystem can easily be converted to ext3*. Generally regarded as a good choice for /boot/.

2. **ext3** *Third Extended Filesystem*- Essentially the ext2 system, but with journaling support. ext3 is completely compatible with ext2. *Extremely* stable, mature, and by far the most widely used, supported and developed GNU/Linux FS.

High Performance Filesystems:

3. **ext4** *Fourth Extended Filesystem*- Backward compatible with ext2 and ext3, Introduces support for volumes with sizes up to 1 exabyte and files with sizes up to 16 terabyte. Increases the 32,000

Part I: Install the Base System

subdirectory limit in ext3 to 64,000. Offers online defragmentation ability.

Note: ext4 is a new filesystem and may have some bugs.

4. **ReiserFS** (V3)- Hans Reiser's high-performance journaling FS uses a very interesting method of data throughput based on an unconventional and creative algorithm. ReiserFS is touted as very fast, especially when dealing with many small files. ReiserFS is fast at formatting, yet comparatively slow at mounting. Quite mature and stable. ReiserFS is not actively developed at this time (Reiser4 is the new Reiser filesystem). Generally regarded as a good choice for /var/.

5. **JFS** - IBM's **J**ournaled **F**ile**S**ystem- The first filesystem to offer journaling. JFS had many years of use in the IBM AIX® OS before being ported to Linux. JFS currently uses the least CPU resources of any GNU/Linux filesystem. Very fast at formatting, mounting and fsck's, and very good all-around performance, especially in conjunction with the deadline I/O scheduler. (See JFS.) Not as widely supported as ext or ReiserFS, but very mature and stable.

6. **XFS** - Another early journaling filesystem originally developed by Silicon Graphics for the IRIX OS and ported to Linux. XFS offers very fast throughput on large files and large filesystems. Very fast at formatting and mounting. Generally benchmarked as slower with many small files, in comparison to other filesystems. XFS is very mature and offers online defragmentation ability.

- JFS and XFS filesystems cannot be *shrunk* by disk utilities (such as gparted or parted magic)

A note on Journaling

All above filesystems, except ext2, use journaling. Journaling file systems are fault-resilient file systems that use a journal to log changes before they are committed to the file system to avoid metadata corruption in the event of a crash. Note that not all journaling techniques are alike; specifically, only ext3 and ext4 offer *data-mode journaling*, (though, not by default), which journals

Arch Linux Handbook

both data *and* meta-data (but with a significant speed penalty). The others only offer *ordered-mode journaling,* which journals meta-data only. While all will return your filesystem to a valid state after recovering from a crash, *data-mode journaling* offers the greatest protection against file system corruption and data loss but can suffer from performance degradation, as all data is written twice (first to the journal, then to the disk). Depending upon how important your data is, this may be a consideration in choosing your filesystem type.

Moving on...

Choose and create the filesystem (format the partition) for / by selecting **yes**. You will now be prompted to add any additional partitions. In our example, sda2 and sda4 remain. For sda2, choose a filesystem type and mount it as /var. Finally, choose the filesystem type for sda4, and mount it as /home. Return to main menu.

D: Select Packages

Now we shall select packages to install in our system.

- Core ISO: Choose CD as source and select the appropriate CD drive if you have more than one.
- FTP ISO: Select an FTP/HTTP mirror. *Note that archlinux.org is throttled to 50KB/s.*

Package selection is split into two stages. First, select the package category:

> **Note**: For expedience, all packages in base are selected by default

- **Base**: The minimal base environment. *Always select it and only remove packages that you don't use.*
- **Base-devel**: Extra tools such as **make, automake** and **wireless-tools** as well as wireless firmwares. *Most beginners should choose to install it, and will probably need it later.*

Part I: Install the Base System

After category selection, you will be presented with the full lists of packages, allowing you to fine-tune your selections. Use the space bar to select and unselect.

> **Note**: If you are going to require connection to a wireless network with WPA encryption, consider installing netcfg2 (as well as wireless_tools), which will enable you to do so.

Once you're done selecting the packages you need, leave the selection screen and continue to the next step, Install Packages.

E: Install Packages

Next, choose 'Install Packages'. You will be asked if you wish to keep the packages in the pacman cache. If you choose 'yes', you will have the flexibility to downgrade to previous package versions in the future, so this is recommended (you can always clear the cache in the future). The installer script will now install the selected packages, as well as the default Arch 2.6 kernel, to your system.

- FTP ISO: The Pacman package manager will now download and install your selected packages. (See vc/5 for output, vc/1 to return to the installer)
- CORE ISO: The packages will be installed from the CD.

F: Configure the System

Closely following and understanding these steps is of key importance to ensure a properly configured system.

At this stage of the installation, you will configure the primary configuration files of your Arch Linux base system.

Previous versions of the installer included hwdetect to gather information for your configuration. This has been deprecated, and udev should handle most module loading automatically at boot.

25

Arch Linux Handbook

The initramfs

The initial ram filesystem, or initramfs, is a temporary file system used by the kernel during boot. It is used for making preparations, like hardware detection and module loading, before the real root file system can be mounted. Therefore, an initramfs allows for the use of a generic modular kernel for a wide variety of hardware, and without the need to compile a custom kernel for each end user.

You will be prompted by a series of questions related to the configuration of your initramfs. You will be asked if you need support for booting from USB devices, FireWire devices, PCMCIA devices, NFS shares, software RAID arrays, LVM2 volumes, encrypted volumes, and DSDT support. Choose yes if you need it; in our example nothing is needed. Choosing 'yes' for any of the above will cause the installer script to place the appropriate hook(s) within the `/etc/mkinitcpio.conf` file.

Now you will be asked which text editor you want to use; choose nano or, if you are familiar with it, vim. You will be presented with a menu including the main configuration files for your system.

> **Note**: It is very important at this point to edit, or at least verify by opening, every configuration file. The installer script relies on your input to create these files on your installation. A common error is to skip over these critical steps of configuration.

Can the installer handle this more automatically?

Hiding the process of system configuration is in direct opposition to The Arch Way. While it is true that recent versions of the kernel and hardware probing tools offer excellent hardware support and auto-configuration, Arch presents the user all pertinent configuration files during installation for the purposes of *transparency and system resource control*. By the time you have finished modifying these files to your specifications, you will have learned the simple method of manual Arch Linux system configuration and become more familiar with the base structure,

26

Part I: Install the Base System

leaving you better prepared to use and maintain your new installation productively.

/etc/rc.conf

Arch Linux uses the file **/etc/rc.conf** as the principal location for system configuration. This one file contains a wide range of configuration information, principally used at system startup. As its name directly implies, it also contains settings for and invokes the /etc/rc* files, and is, of course, sourced *by* these files.

LOCALIZATION section

- **LOCALE**=: This sets your system locale, which will be used by all i18n-aware applications and utilities. You can get a list of the available locales by running 'locale -a' from the command line. This setting's default is fine for US English users.
- **HARDWARECLOCK**=: Specifies whether the hardware clock, which is synchronized on boot and on shutdown, stores **UTC** time, or the **localtime**. UTC makes sense because it greatly simplifies changing timezones and daylight savings time. localtime is necessary if you dual boot with an operating system such as Windows, that only stores localtime to the hardware clock.
- **USEDIRECTISA**: Use direct I/O request instead of /dev/rtc for hwclock
- **TIMEZONE**=: Specify your TIMEZONE. (All available zones are under /usr/share/zoneinfo/).
- **KEYMAP**=: The available keymaps are in /usr/share/kbd/keymaps. Please note that this setting is only valid for your TTYs, not any graphical window managers or **X**.
- **CONSOLEFONT**=: Available console fonts reside under /usr/share/kbd/consolefonts/ if you must change. The default (blank) is safe.
- **CONSOLEMAP**=: Defines the console map to load with the setfont program at boot. Possible maps are found in

27

Arch Linux Handbook

/usr/share/kbd/consoletrans, if needed. The default (blank) is safe.

- **USECOLOR**=: Select "yes" if you have a color monitor and wish to have colors in your consoles.

```
LOCALE="en_US.utf8"
HARDWARECLOCK="localtime"
USEDIRECTISA="no"
TIMEZONE="US/Eastern"
KEYMAP="us"
CONSOLEFONT=
CONSOLEMAP=
USECOLOR="yes"
```

HARDWARE Section

- **MOD_AUTOLOAD**=: Setting this to "yes" will use **udev** to automatically probe hardware and load the appropriate modules during boot-up, (convenient with the default modular kernel). Setting this to "no" will rely on the user's ability to specify this information manually, or compile their own custom kernel and modules, etc.
- **MOD_BLACKLIST**=: This has become deprecated in favor of adding blacklisted modules directly to the **MODULES=** line below.
- **MODULES**=: Specify additional MODULES if you know that an important module is missing. If your system has any floppy drives, add "floppy". If you will be using loopback filesystems, add "loop". Also specify any blacklisted modules by prefixing them with a bang (!). Udev will be forced NOT to load blacklisted modules. In the example, the IPv6 module as well as the annoying pcspeaker are blacklisted.

Part I: Install the Base System

```
# Scan hardware and load required modules at boot
MOD_AUTOLOAD="yes"
# Module Blacklist - Deprecated
MOD_BLACKLIST=()
#
MODULES=(!net-pf-10 !snd_pcsp !pcspkr loop)
```

NETWORKING Section

- **HOSTNAME**=:Set your HOSTNAME to your liking.
- **eth0**=: 'Ethernet, card 0'. Adjust the interface IP address, netmask and broadcast address *if* you are using **static IP**. Set eth0="dhcp" if you want to use **DHCP**
- **INTERFACES**=: Specify all interfaces here.
- **gateway**=: If you are using **static IP**, set the gateway address. If using **DHCP**, you can usually ignore this variable, though some users have reported the need to define it.
- **ROUTES**=: If you are using static **IP**, remove the **!** in front of 'gateway'. If using **DHCP**, you can usually leave this variable commented out with the bang (!), but again, some users require the gateway and ROUTES defined. If you experience networking issues with pacman, for instance, you may want to return to these variables.

29

Arch Linux Handbook

Example, using a dynamically assigned IP address (DHCP)

```
HOSTNAME="arch"
#eth0="eth0 192.168.0.2 netmask 255.255.255.0 broadcast
192.168.0.255"
eth0="dhcp"
INTERFACES=(eth0)
gateway="default gw 192.168.0.1"
ROUTES=(!gateway)
```

Note: Arch uses the dhcpcd DHCP client. Alternatively, dhclient is available from the [extra] repository via pacman.

Example, using a static IP address

```
HOSTNAME="arch"
eth0="eth0 192.168.0.2 netmask 255.255.255.0 broadcast
192.168.0.255"
INTERFACES=(eth0)
gateway="default gw 192.168.0.1"
ROUTES=(gateway)
```

Tip: If you also require using a non-standard MTU size (a.k.a. jumbo frames) to speed up intranet xfers AND your hardware supports them, see the Jumbo Frames wiki article for further configuration.

Note: In some cases, users will need to modify their /etc/reslov.conf to prevent the dhcpcd daemon from overwriting the DNS entries.

Modify your /etc/reslov.conf to contain lines to your the DNS's that your ISP uses.

30

Part I: Install the Base System

```
search my.ips.net.
nameserver a.b.c.d
nameserver a.b.c.d
nameserver a.b.c.d
```

> **Tip:** If you are unsure what values to use in the
> /etc/reslov.conf simply configure your system to use
> DHCP and look at the /etc/reslov.conf which should be
> automatically set for you. You may use these values.

Finally, /etc/conf.d/dhcpcd needs to be tweaked to keep the
dhcpcd from overwriting your /etc/reslov.conf which will
happen without this modification:

```
# Arguments to be passed to the DHCP client daemon
#

# DHCPCD_ARGS="-q"
DHCPCD_ARGS="-C resolv.conf -q"
```

DAEMONS Section

This array simply lists the names of those scripts contained in
/etc/rc.d/ which are to be started during the boot process, and the
order in which they start.

```
DAEMONS=(network @syslog-ng netfs @crond)
```

- If a script name is prefixed with a bang (!), it is not
  executed.
- If a script is prefixed with an "at" symbol (@), it shall be
  executed in the background; the startup sequence will not
  wait for successful completion of each daemon before
  continuing to the next. (Useful for speeding up system
  boot). Do not background daemons that are needed by other

31

Arch Linux Handbook

daemons. For example "mpd" depends on "network", therefore backgrounding network may cause mpd to break.

- Edit this array whenever new system services are installed, if starting them automatically during boot is desired.

This 'BSD-style' init, is the Arch way of handling what other distributions handle with various symlinks to an /etc/init.d directory.

About DAEMONS

You do not have to change the daemons line at this time, but it is useful to explain what daemons are, because we need them later in this guide. A *daemon* is a program that runs in the background, waiting for events to occur and offering services. A good example is a webserver that waits for a request to deliver a page or an SSH server waiting for someone trying to log in. While these are full-featured applications, there are daemons whose work is not that visible. Examples are a daemon which writes messages into a log file (e.g. syslog, metalog), a daemon which lowers your CPU's frequency if your system has nothing to do (e.g.:cpufreq), and a daemon which offers you a graphical login (e.g.: gdm, kdm). All these programs can be added to the daemons line and will be started when the system boots. Useful daemons will be presented during this guide.

Historically, the term *daemon* was coined by the programmers of MIT's Project MAC. They took the name from *Maxwell's demon*, an imaginary being from a famous thought experiment that constantly works in the background, sorting molecules. UNIX systems inherited this terminology and created the backronym **d**isk **a**nd **e**xecution **mon**itor.

> **Tip**: All Arch daemons reside under /etc/rc.d/

/etc/fstab

The **fstab** (for **f**ile **s**ystems **tab**le) is part of the system configuration listing all available disks and disk partitions, and indicating how they are to be initialized or otherwise integrated into the overall

Part I: Install the Base System

system's filesystem. The **/etc/fstab** file is most commonly used by the **mount** command. The mount command takes a filesystem on a device, and adds it to the main system hierarchy that you see when you use your system. **mount -a** is called from /etc/rc.sysinit, about 3/4 of the way through the boot process, and reads /etc/fstab to determine which options should be used when mounting the specified devices therein. If **noauto** is appended to a filesystem in /etc/fstab, **mount -a** will not mount it at boot.

An example /etc/fstab

```
# <file system>          <dir>          <type>
<options>                   <dump>       <pass>
none                     /dev/pts        devpts
defaults                     0              0
none                     /dev/shm        tmpfs
defaults                     0              0
#/dev/cdrom              /media/cdrom    auto
ro,user,noauto,unhide        0              0
#/dev/dvd                /media/dvd      auto
ro,user,noauto,unhide        0              0
#/dev/fd0                /media/fl       auto
user,noauto                  0              0
/dev/disk/by-uuid/0ec-933.. /            jfs
defaults,noatime             0              1
/dev/disk/by-uuid/7ef-223.. /home        jfs
defaults,noatime             0              2
/dev/disk/by-uuid/530-1e-.. swap         swap
defaults                     0              0
/dev/disk/by-uuid/4fe-110.. /var         reiserfs
defaults,noatime,notail      0              2
```

Note: The 'noatime' option disables writing read access times to the metadata of files and may safely be appended to / and /home regardless of your specified filesystem type for increased speed, performance, and power efficiency. 'notail' disables the ReiserFS tailpacking feature, for added performance at the cost of slightly less efficient disk usage.

Arch Linux Handbook

> **Note:** It may be beneficial to make a note of the UUID of the root (/) partition, as this may be required during GRUB configuration.

- **<file system>**: describes the block device or remote filesystem to be mounted. For regular mounts, this field will contain a link to a block device node (as created by mknod which is called by udev at boot) for the device to be mounted; for instance, '/dev/cdrom' or '/dev/sda1'. Instead of giving the device explicitly, the Arch installer indicates the filesystem that is to be mounted by its UUID by default.

> **Note:** As of 2008-04rc, Arch is now utilizing the UUID, or Universally Unique Identifier naming convention, for consistent device mapping. This is due to active developments in the kernel and also udev, which may randomly change the ordering in which drivers for storage controllers are loaded, yielding an unbootable system/kernel panic. Nearly every motherboard has several controllers (onboard SATA, onboard IDE), and due to the aforementioned development updates, /dev/sda may become /dev/sdb on the next reboot- hence the persistent device naming convention of UUID has been adopted for reliability. *If you do not need nor wish to use UUID, simply change your fstab to use whatever naming convention desired.* (See this wiki article for more information on persistent block device naming.)

```
ls -lF /dev/disk/by-uuid/
```

will list all partitions by UUID, while

Part I: Install the Base System

```
/sbin/blkid
```

will show a list correlating each partition with its label, filesystem type and UUID. *Note: this command is installed by the **e2fsprogs** package.*

- **<dir>**: describes the mount point for the filesystem. For swap partitions, this field should be specified as 'swap'; (Swap partitions are not actually mounted.)

- **<type>**: describes the type of the filesystem. The Linux kernel supports many filesystem types. (For the filesystems currently supported by the running kernel, see /proc/filesystems). An entry 'swap' denotes a file or partition to be used for swapping. An entry 'ignore' causes the line to be ignored. This is useful to show disk partitions which are currently unused.

- **<options>**: describes the mount options associated with the filesystem. It is formatted as a comma separated list of options with no intervening spaces. It contains at least the type of mount plus any additional options appropriate to the filesystem type. For documentation on the available options for non-nfs file systems, see mount(8).

- **<dump>**: used by the dump(8) command to determine which filesystems are to be dumped. dump is a backup utility. If the fifth field is not present, a value of zero is returned and dump will assume that the filesystem does not need to be backed up. *Note that dump is not installed by default.*

- **<pass>**: used by the fsck(8) program to determine the order in which filesystem checks are done at boot time. The root filesystem should be specified with a <pass> of 1, and other filesystems should have a <pass> of 2 or 0. Filesystems within a drive will be checked sequentially, but filesystems on different drives will be checked at the same time to utilize parallelism available in the hardware. If the sixth field is not present or zero, a value of zero is returned and

Arch Linux Handbook

fsck will assume that the filesystem does not need to be checked.

- If you plan on using **hal** to automount media such as DVDs, you may wish to comment out the cdrom and dvd entries in preparation for **hal**, which will be installed later in this guide.

Expanded information available in the Fstab wiki entry.

/etc/mkinitcpio.conf

This file allows you to fine-tune the initial ram filesystem (also commonly referred to as the initial ramdisk or "initrd") for your system. The initrd is a gzipped image that is read by the kernel during boot. The purpose of the initrd is to bootstrap the system to the point where it can access the root filesystem. This means it has to load any modules that are required for devices like IDE, SCSI, or SATA drives (or USB/FW, if you are booting off a USB/FW drive). Once the initrd loads the proper modules, either manually or through udev, it passes control to the Arch system and your boot continues. For this reason, the initrd only needs to contain the modules necessary to access the root filesystem. It does not need to contain every module you would ever want to use. The majority of your everyday modules will be loaded later on by udev, during the init process.

mkinitcpio is the next generation of **initramfs creation**. It has many advantages over the old **mkinitrd** and **mkinitramfs** scripts.

- It uses **klibc** and **kinit** which are developed by Linux kernel devs to provide a small and lightweight base for early userspace.
- It can use **udev** for hardware autodetection at runtime, thus prevents you from having tons of unnecessary modules loaded.
- Its hook-based init script is easily extendable with custom hooks, which can easily be included in pacman packages without having to modifiy mkinitcpio itself.

36

Part I: Install the Base System

- It already supports **lvm2, dm-crypt** for both legacy and luks volumes, **raid, swsusp** and **suspend2** resuming and booting from **usb mass storage** devices.
- Many features can be configured from the kernel command line without having to rebuild the image.
- The **mkinitcpio** script makes it possible to include the image in a kernel, thus making a self-contained kernel image is possible.
- Its flexibility makes recompiling a kernel unnecessary in many cases.

If you are using a non-US keyboard you may want to add "keymap" to the "HOOKS=" section of **/etc/mkinitcpio.conf** to load your local keymap during boot, e.g.:

```
HOOKS="base udev autodetect pata scsi sata filesystems
keymap"
```

Otherwise if boot fails for some reason you will be asked to enter root's password for system maintenance but will be unable to do so.

If you are using a US keyboard editing this configuration should be unnecessary at this point.

mkinitcpio was developed by Aaron Griffin and Tobias Powalowski with some help from the community.

/etc/modprobe.conf

It is unnecessary to configure this file at this time.

- **modprobe.conf** can be used to set special configuration options for the kernel modules

Note: The new module-init-tools 3.8 package changes the location of the configuration file: /etc/modprobe.conf is no longer read, instead /etc/modprobe.d/modprobe.conf is used. link

Arch Linux Handbook

/etc/resolv.conf (for Static IP)

The *resolver* is a set of routines in the C library that provide access to the Internet Domain Name System (DNS). One of the main functions of DNS is to translate domain names into IP addresses, to make the Web a friendlier place. The resolver configuration file, or /etc/resolv.conf, contains information that is read by the resolver routines the first time they are invoked by a process.

> • *If you are using DHCP, you may safely ignore this file, as by default, it will be dynamically created and destroyed by the dhcpcd daemon. You may change this default behavior if you wish. (See Network]).*

If you use a static IP, set your DNS servers in /etc/resolv.conf (nameserver <ip-address>). You may have as many as you wish. An example, using OpenDNS:

```
nameserver 208.67.222.222
nameserver 208.67.220.220
```

If you are using a router, you will probably want to specify your DNS servers in the router itself, and merely point to it from your **/etc/resolv.conf**, using your router's IP (which is also your gateway from **/etc/rc.conf**), e.g.:

```
nameserver 192.168.1.1
```

If using **DHCP**, you may also specify your DNS servers in the router, or allow automatic assignment from your ISP, if your ISP is so equipped.

/etc/hosts

This file associates IP addresses with hostnames and aliases, one line per IP address. For each host a single line should be present with the following information:

Part I: Install the Base System

```
<IP-address> <hostname> [aliases...]
```

Add your *hostname*, coinciding with the one specified in /etc/rc.conf, as an alias, so that it looks like this:

```
127.0.0.1    localhost.localdomain    localhost
yourhostname
```

This format, **including the 'localhost' and your actual host name**, is required for program compatibility! So, if you have named your computer Archhost, then that line above should look like this:

```
127.0.0.1    localhost.localdomain    localhost Archhost
```

Errors in this entry may cause poor network performance and/or certain programs to open very slowly, or not work at all. This is a very common error for beginners.

If you use a static IP, add another line using the syntax: <static-IP> <hostname.domainname.org> <hostname> e.g.:

```
192.168.1.100 yourhostname.domain.org  yourhostname
```

Tip: For convenience, you may also use /etc/hosts aliases for hosts on your network, and/or on the Web, e.g.:

```
64.233.169.103   www.google.com    g
192.168.1.90     media
192.168.1.88     data
```

The above example would allow you to access google simply by typing 'g' into your browser, and access to a media and data server on your network by name and without the need for typing out their respective IP addresses.

39

Arch Linux Handbook

/etc/hosts.deny and /etc/hosts.allow

Modify these configurations according to your needs if you plan on using the ssh daemon. The default configuration will reject all incoming connections, not only ssh connections. Edit your **/etc/hosts.allow** file and add the appropriate parameters:

- let everyone connect to you

```
sshd: ALL
```

- restrict it to a certain ip

```
sshd: 192.168.0.1
```

- restrict it to your local LAN network (range 192.168.0.0 to 192.168.0.255)

```
sshd: 192.168.0.
```

- OR restrict for an IP range

```
sshd: 10.0.0.0/255.255.255.0
```

If you do not plan on using the ssh daemon, leave this file at the default, (empty), for added security.

/etc/locale.gen

The **/usr/sbin/locale-gen** command reads from **/etc/locale.gen** to generate specific locales. They can then be used by **glibc** and any other locale-aware program or library for rendering "peculiar" text, correctly displaying regional monetary values, time and date formats, alphabetic idiosyncrasies, and other locale-specific standards. The ability to setup a default locale is a great built-in privilege of using a UNIX-like operating system.

Part I: Install the Base System

By default /etc/locale.gen is an empty file with commented documentation. Once edited, the file remains untouched. **locale-gen** runs on every **glibc** upgrade, generating all the locales specified in /etc/locale.gen.

Choose the locale(s) you need (remove the # in front of the lines you want), e.g.:

```
en_US ISO-8859-1
en_US.UTF-8
```

The installer will now run the locale-gen script, which will generate the locales you specified. You may change your locale in the future by editing /etc/locale.gen and subsequently running 'locale-gen' as root.

> Note: *If you fail to choose your locale, this will lead to a "The current locale is invalid..." error. This is perhaps the most common mistake by new Arch users, and also leads to the most commonly asked questions on the forum.*

Root password

Finally, set a root password and make sure that you remember it later. Return to the main menu and continue with installing bootloader.

Pacman-Mirror

Choose a mirror repository for **pacman**.

- *archlinux.org is throttled, limiting downloads to 50KB/s*

Return to the main menu.

Arch Linux Handbook

G: Install Bootloader

Because we have no secondary operating system in our example, we will need a bootloader. GNU GRUB is the recommended bootloader. Alternatively, you may choose LILO.

GRUB

The provided **GRUB** configuration (**/boot/grub/menu.lst**) should be sufficient, but verify its contents to ensure accuracy (specifically, ensure that the root (/) partition is specified by UUID on line 3). You may want to alter the resolution of the console by adding a vga=<number> kernel argument corresponding to your desired virtual console resolution. (A table of resolutions and the corresponding numbers is printed in the menu.lst.)

Example:

```
title   Arch Linux (Main)
root    (hd0,0)
kernel /boot/vmlinuz26 root=/dev/disk/by-uuid/0ec1-
9339.. ro vga=773
initrd /boot/kernel26.img
```

Note: *The linux kernel, 'vmlinuz', is so named because it incorporated virtual memory capability early in its development. The z denotes a zipped (compressed) image.*

Explanation:

Line 1: **title**: A printed menu selection. "Arch Linux (Main)" will be printed on the screen as a menu selection.

Line 2: **root**: **GRUB**'s root; the drive and partition where the kernel (/boot) resides, according to system BIOS. (More accurately, where GRUB's stage2 file resides). **NOT necessarily the root** (/) file system, as they can reside on separate partitions. GRUB's numbering scheme starts at 0, and uses an hd*x,x* format regardless of IDE or SATA, and enclosed within parentheses.

42

Part I: Install the Base System

The example indicates that /boot is on the first partition of the first drive, according to BIOS, or, (hd0,0).

Line 3: **kernel**: This line specifies:

- The path and filename of the kernel *relative to GRUB's root*.

In the example, /boot is merely a directory residing on the same partition as / and **vmlinuz26** is the kernel filename; **/boot/vmlinuz26**. *If /boot were on a separate partition, the path and filename would be simply /vmlinuz26, being relative to GRUB's root.*

- The root= argument to the kernel statement specifies the partition containing the root (/) directory in the booted system, (more accurately, the partition containing **/sbin/init**). If not already specified, you should enter the name of the partition, according to the UUID numbering scheme, using the */dev/disk/by-uuid/xxxx-xxxx-xxxx* format. This UUID was found in the previous section regarding configuration of */etc/fstab*.

- An easy way to distinguish the 2 appearances of 'root' in /boot/grub/menu.lst is to remember that the first root statement *informs GRUB where the kernel resides*, whereas the second root= kernel argument *tells the kernel where the root filesystem (/) resides*.

- Kernel options.

In our example, **ro** mounts the filesystem as read only during startup, and the **"vga=773"** argument will give a 1024x768 framebuffer with 256 color depth.

Line 4: **initrd**: (For Initial RAM disk) The path and filename of the initial RAM filesystem **relative to GRUB's** root. Again, in the example, /boot is merely a directory residing on the same partition as / and **kernel26.img** is the initrd filename; **/boot/kernel26.img**. *If /boot were on a separate partition, the path and filename would be simply /kernel26.img, being relative to GRUB's root.*

Install the **GRUB** bootloader (to the master boot record, sda in our example).

43

Arch Linux Handbook

> **Tip:** For more details, see the GRUB wiki page.

H: Reboot

That's it; You have configured and installed your Arch Linux base system. Exit the install, and reboot:

```
# reboot
```

(Be sure to remove the installer CD)

Part II: Configure&Update the New Arch Linux base system

Part II: Configure&Update the New Arch Linux base system

Your new Arch Linux system will boot up and finish with a login prompt (you may want to change the boot order in your **BIOS** back to booting from hard disk).

Congratulations, and welcome to your new Arch Linux base system!

Your new Arch Linux base system is now a functional GNU/Linux environment ready for customization. From here, you may build this elegant set of tools into whatever you wish or require for your purposes.

Login with the root account. We will configure pacman and update the system as root, then add a normal user.

> **Note:** Virtual consoles 1-6 are available. You may swap between them with ALT+F1...F6

Step 1: Configuring the network (if necessary)

- *This section will assist you in configuring most types of networks, if your network configuration is not working for you.*

If you properly configured your system, you should have a working network. Try to ping www.google.com to verify this.

```
# ping -c 3 www.google.com
```

*If you have successfully established a network connection, continue with **Update, Sync and Upgrade the system with pacman.***

If, after trying to ping www.google.com, an "unknown host" error is received, you may conclude that your network is not properly

45

Arch Linux Handbook

configured. You may choose to double-check the following files for integrity and proper settings:

/etc/rc.conf # Specifically, check your HOSTNAME= and NETWORKING section for typos and errors.

/etc/hosts # Double-check your format. (See above.)

/etc/resolv.conf # If you are using a static IP. If you are using DHCP, this file will be dynamically created and destroyed by default, but can be changed to your preference. (See Network.)

> **Tip:** Advanced instructions for configuring the network can be found in the Network article.

Wired LAN

Check your Ethernet with

```
# ifconfig -a
```

All interfaces will be listed. You should see an entry for eth0, or perhaps eth1.

- **Static IP**

If required, you can set a new static IP with:

```
# ifconfig eth0 <ip address> netmask <netmask> up
```

and the default gateway with

```
# route add default gw <ip address of the gateway>
```

Verify that /etc/resolv.conf contains your DNS server and add it if it is missing. Check your network again with ping www.google.com. If everything is working now, adjust /etc/rc.conf as described above for static IP.

46

Part II: Configure&Update the New Arch Linux base system

- ## **DHCP**

If you have a DHCP server/router in your network try:

```
# dhcpcd eth0
```

If this is working, adjust /etc/rc.conf as described above, for dynamic IP.

Wireless LAN

- Ensure the driver has created a usable interface:

```
# iwconfig
```

- Bring the interface up with `ifconfig <interface> up`. e.g.:

```
# ifconfig wlan0 up
```

- (Optional) Scan for available access points:

```
# iwlist wlan0 scan | less
```

- Specify the id of the wireless network with `iwconfig <interface> essid <youressid>`. Or, if using WEP; `iwconfig <interface> essid <youressid> key <yourwepkey>`, e.g.:

```
# iwconfig wlan0 essid linksys key ABCDEF01234
```

- Request an IP address with `dhcpcd <interface>`. e.g.:

47

Arch Linux Handbook

```
# dhcpcd wlan0
```

- Ensure you can route:

```
$ ping -c 3 www.google.com
```

Done.

Detailed setup guide: Wireless Setup

Analog Modem

To be able to use a Hayes-compatible, external, analog modem, you need to at least have the ppp package installed. Modify the file /etc/ppp/options to suit your needs and according to man pppd. You will need to define a chat script to supply your username and password to the ISP after the initial connection has been established. The manpages for pppd and chat have examples in them that should suffice to get a connection up and running if you're either experienced or stubborn enough. With udev, your serial ports usually are /dev/tts/0 and /dev/tts/1.

Instead of fighting a glorious battle with the plain pppd, you may opt to install wvdial or a similar tool to ease the setup process considerably. In case you're using a so-called WinModem, which is basically a PCI plugin card working as an internal analog modem, you should indulge in the vast information found on the LinModem homepage.

ISDN

Setting up ISDN is done in three steps:

1. Install and configure hardware
2. Install and configure the ISDN utilities
3. Add settings for your ISP

The current Arch stock kernels include the necessary ISDN modules, meaning that you will not need to recompile your kernel

Part II: Configure&Update the New Arch Linux base system

unless you're about to use rather odd ISDN hardware. After physically installing your ISDN card in your machine or plugging in your USB ISDN-Box, you can try loading the modules with modprobe. Nearly all passive ISDN PCI cards are handled by the hisax module, which needs two parameters: type and protocol. You must set protocol to '1' if your country uses the 1TR6 standard, '2' if it uses EuroISDN (EDSS1), '3' if you're hooked to a so-called leased-line without D-channel, and '4' for US NI1.

Details on all those settings and how to set them is included in the kernel documentation, more specifically in the isdn subdirectory, and available online. The type parameter depends on your card; a list of all possible types can be found in the README.HiSax kernel documentation. Choose your card and load the module with the appropriate options like this:

```
# modprobe hisax type=18 protocol=2
```

This will load the hisax module for my ELSA Quickstep 1000PCI, being used in Germany with the EDSS1 protocol. You should find helpful debugging output in your /var/log/everything.log file, in which you should see your card being prepared for action. Please note that you will probably need to load some USB modules before you can work with an external USB ISDN Adapter.

Once you have confirmed that your card works with certain settings, you can add the module options to your /etc/modprobe.conf:

```
alias ippp0 hisax
options hisax type=18 protocol=2
```

Alternatively, you can add only the options line here, and add hisax to your MODULES array in the rc.conf. It's your choice, really, but this example has the advantage that the module will not be loaded until it's really needed.

That being done, you should have working, supported hardware. Now you need the basic utilities to actually use it!

49

Arch Linux Handbook

Install the isdn4k-utils package, and read the manpage to isdnctrl; it'll get you started. Further down in the manpage you will find explanations on how to create a configuration file that can be parsed by isdnctrl, as well as some helpful setup examples. Please note that you have to add your SPID to your MSN setting separated by a colon if you use US NI1.

After you have configured your ISDN card with the isdnctrl utility, you should be able to dial into the machine you specified with the PHONE_OUT parameter, but fail the username and password authentication. To make this work add your username and password to /etc/ppp/pap-secrets or /etc/ppp/chap-secrets as if you were configuring a normal analogous PPP link, depending on which protocol your ISP uses for authentication. If in doubt, put your data into both files.

If you set up everything correctly, you should now be able to establish a dial-up connection with

```
# isdnctrl dial ippp0
```

as root. If you have any problems, remember to check the logfiles!

DSL (PPPoE)

These instructions are relevant to you only if your PC itself is supposed to manage the connection to your ISP. You do not need to do anything but define a correct default gateway if you are using a separate router of some sort to do the grunt work.

Before you can use your DSL online connection, you will have to physically install the network card that is supposed to be connected to the DSL-Modem into your computer. After adding your newly installed network card to the modules.conf/modprobe.conf or the MODULES array, you should install the rp-pppoe package and run the pppoe-setup script to configure your connection. After you have entered all the data, you can connect and disconnect your line with

Part II: Configure&Update the New Arch Linux base
system

```
# /etc/rc.d/adsl start
```

and

```
# /etc/rc.d/adsl stop
```

respectively. The setup usually is rather easy and straightforward, but feel free to read the manpages for hints. If you want to automatically 'dial in' on boot-up, add adsl to your DAEMONS array, and put a ! before the network entry, since the network is handled by adsl now.

Step 2: Update, Sync and Upgrade the system with pacman

Now we will update the system using pacman.

What is pacman ?

Pacman is the **pac**kage **man**ager of Arch Linux. Pacman is written in *C* and is designed from the ground up to be lightweight with a very modest memory footprint, fast, simple, and versatile. It manages your entire package system and handles installation, removal, package downgrade (through cache), custom compiled package handling, automatic dependency resolution, remote and local searches and much more. Pacman's output is streamlined, very readable and provides ETA for each package download. Arch uses the .tar.gz package format, which further enhances pacman's speed; Gzipped tarballs, though slightly larger, are decompressed many times faster than their Bzipped counterparts, and are therefore installed much more expediently.

We will use pacman to download software packages from remote repositories and install them onto your system.

51

Arch Linux Handbook

Pacman is the most important tool in your Arch Linux toolbox for building the base system into whatsoever you please.

Package Repositories and /etc/pacman.conf

Arch currently offers the following 4 repositories readily accessible through pacman:

[core]

The simple principle behind [core] is to provide only one of each necessary tool for a base Arch Linux system; The GNU toolchain, the Linux kernel, one editor, one command line browser, etc. (There are a few exceptions to this. For instance, both vi and nano are provided, allowing the user to choose one or both.) It contains all the packages that MUST be in perfect working order to ensure the system remains in a usable state. These are the absolute system-critical packages.

- Developer maintained
- All binary packages
- pacman accessible
- *The Core installation media simply contains an installer script, and a snapshot of the core repository at the time of release.*

[extra]

The [extra] repository contains all Arch packages that are not themselves necessary for a base Arch system, but contribute to a more full-featured environment. **X**, KDE, and Apache, for instance, can be found here.

- Developer maintained
- All binary packages
- pacman accessible

[testing]

The [testing] repository contains packages that are candidates for the [core] or [extra] repositories. New packages go into [testing] if:

Part II: Configure&Update the New Arch Linux base system

* they are expected to break something on update and need to be tested first.

* they require other packages to be rebuilt. In this case, all packages that need to be rebuilt are put into [testing] first and when all rebuilds are done, they are moved back to the other repositories.

- Developer maintained
- All binary packages
- pacman accessible

Note: * [testing] is the only repository that can have name collisions with any of the other official repositories. Therefore, if enabled, [testing] must be the first repo listed in `pacman.conf`.

Warning: Only experienced users should use [testing].

[community]

The [community] repository is maintained by the *Trusted Users (TUs)* and is simply the binary branch of the *Arch User Repository (AUR)*. It contains binary packages which originated as PKGBUILDs from *AUR* [unsupported] that have acquired enough votes and were adopted by a *TU*. Like all repos listed above, [community] may be readily accessed by pacman.

- TU maintained
- All binary packages
- pacman accessible

AUR (unsupported)

The **AUR** also contains the **unsupported** branch, which cannot be accessed directly by pacman*. **AUR** [unsupported] does not contain binary packages. Rather, it provides more than sixteen thousand PKGBUILD scripts for building packages from source, that may be unavailable through the other repos. When an AUR unsupported

53

Arch Linux Handbook

package acquires enough popular votes, it may be moved to the AUR [community] binary repo, if a TU is willing to adopt and maintain it there.

- TU maintained
- All PKGBUILD bash build scripts
- *Not* pacman accessible by default

* pacman wrappers (*AUR Helpers*) can help you seamlessly access AUR.

/etc/pacman.conf

pacman will attempt to read /etc/pacman.conf each time it is invoked. This configuration file is divided into sections, or repositories. Each section defines a package repository that pacman can use when searching for packages. The exception to this is the options section, which defines global options.

```
# nano /etc/pacman.conf
```

Example:

Part II: Configure&Update the New Arch Linux base system

```
#
# /etc/pacman.conf
#
# See the pacman.conf(5) manpage for option and
repository directives

#
# GENERAL OPTIONS
#
[options]
# The following paths are commented out with their
default values listed.
# If you wish to use different paths, uncomment and
update the paths.
#RootDir     = /
#DBPath      = /var/lib/pacman/
#CacheDir    = /var/cache/pacman/pkg/
#LogFile     = /var/log/pacman.log
HoldPkg     = pacman glibc
# If upgrades are available for these packages they will
be asked for first
SyncFirst   = pacman
#XferCommand = /usr/bin/wget --passive-ftp -c -O %o %u
#XferCommand = /usr/bin/curl %u > %o

# Pacman won't upgrade packages listed in IgnorePkg and
members of IgnoreGroup
#IgnorePkg   =
#IgnoreGroup =
```

Arch Linux Handbook

```
#NoUpgrade   =
#NoExtract   =

# Misc options (all disabled by default)
#NoPassiveFtp
#UseSyslog
#ShowSize
#UseDelta
#TotalDownload
#
```

Part II: Configure&Update the New Arch Linux base system

```
# REPOSITORIES
#    - can be defined here or included from another file
#    - pacman will search repositories in the order
defined here
#    - local/custom mirrors can be added here or in
separate files
#    - repositories listed first will take precedence
when packages
#      have identical names, regardless of version number
#    - URLs will have $repo replaced by the name of the
current repo
#
# Repository entries are of the format:
#      [repo-name]
#      Server = ServerName
#      Include = IncludePath
#
# The header [repo-name] is crucial - it must be present
and
# uncommented to enable the repo.
#

# Testing is disabled by default.  To enable, uncomment
the following
# two lines.  You can add preferred servers immediately
after the header,
# and they will be used before the default mirrors.
#[testing]
#Include = /etc/pacman.d/mirrorlist

[core]
# Add your preferred servers here, they will be used
first
Include = /etc/pacman.d/mirrorlist

[extra]
# Add your preferred servers here, they will be used
first
Include = /etc/pacman.d/mirrorlist

[community]
# Add your preferred servers here, they will be used
first
Include = /etc/pacman.d/mirrorlist
```

Arch Linux Handbook

```
# An example of a custom package repository.  See the
pacman manpage for
# tips on creating your own repositories.
#[custom]
#Server = file:///home/custompkgs
```

Enable all desired repositories (remove the # in front of the 'Include
=' and '[repository]' lines).

- *When choosing repos, be sure to uncomment both the
  repository header lines in [brackets] as well as the
  'Include =' lines. Failure to do so will result in the
  selected repository being omitted! This is a very common
  error.*

/etc/pacman.d/mirrorlist

Faster mirrors will dramatically improve pacman performance, and
your overall Arch Linux experience.

Edit /etc/pacman.d/mirrorlist:

- **Manually:**

```
# nano /etc/pacman.d/mirrorlist
```

Remove all mirrors which are not on your continent, or are
extremely distant. In nano, [CTRL]+K will cut each unneeded line.

Edit /etc/pacman.d/mirrorlist by placing the best mirror at the top of
the list. (Recall that archlinux.org is throttled to 50KB/s). In nano,
[ALT]+A selects an area, cursor down marks the lines, [CTRL]+K
cuts the selected area and [CTRL]+U uncuts, or pastes it.

- **Alternative, using the rankmirrors script:**

/usr/bin/rankmirrors is a python script which will attempt
to detect the mirrors which are closest to you.

58

Part II: Configure&Update the New Arch Linux base system

First, use pacman to install python:

```
# pacman -Sy python
```

cd to the /etc/pacman.d/ directory:

```
# cd /etc/pacman.d
```

Backup your existing /etc/pacman.d/mirrorlist:

```
# cp mirrorlist mirrorlist.backup
```

Edit mirrorlist.backup and uncomment mirrors you want to test with rankmirrors.

Run the script against the mirrorlist.backup with the -n switch and redirect output to a new /etc/pacman.d/mirrorlist file:

```
# rankmirrors -n 6 mirrorlist.backup > mirrorlist
```

-n 6: rank the 6 fastest mirrors

Force pacman to refresh the package lists

After creating/editing your /etc/pacman.d/mirrorlist, (manually or by `/usr/bin/rankmirrors`) issue the following command:

```
# pacman -Syy
```

Passing two --refresh or -y flags forces pacman to refresh all package lists even if they are considered to be up to date. Issuing pacman -Syy *whenever a mirror is changed,* is good practice and will avoid possible headaches.

59

Arch Linux Handbook

Mirrorcheck for up-to-date packages

Some of the official mirrors may contain packages that are out-of-date. [ArchLinux Mirrorcheck] reports various aspects about the mirrors such as, those experiencing network problems, data collection problems, reports the last time they have been synced, etc.

One may wish to manually inspect the mirrors in the /etc/pacman.d/mirrorlist insuring that it only contains up-to-date mirrors if having the latest and greatest package versions is important to you.

Ignoring packages

When you execute the command "pacman -Syu", your entire system will be updated. It is possible that you want to prevent a package from being upgraded. An example could be the kernel (kernel26) or a package for which an upgrade may prove problematic for your system. In this case, you have two options; indicate the package(s) you want to skip in the pacman command line using the --ignore switch (do pacman -S --help for details) or permanently indicate the package(s) you want to skip in your /etc/pacman.conf file in the IgnorePkg array. List each package, with one intervening space :

```
IgnorePkg = wine
```

The typical way to use Arch is to use pacman to install all packages unless there is no package available, in which case you can build your own package using ABS. Many user-contributed package build scripts are also available in the AUR.

You are expected to keep your system up to date with pacman -Syu, rather than selectively upgrading packages. You may diverge from this typical usage as you wish; just be warned that there is a greater chance that things will not work as intended and that it could break your system. The majority of complaints happen when selective upgrading, unusual compilation or improper software installation is performed. Use of **IgnorePkg** in /etc/pacman.conf is therefore

60

Part II: Configure&Update the New Arch Linux base
system

discouraged, and should only be used sparingly, if you know what
you are doing.

Ignoring Configuration Files

In the same vein, you can also "protect" your configuration/system
files from being overwritten during "pacman -Su" using the
following option in your /etc/pacman.conf

```
NoUpgrade = etc/lilo.conf boot/grub/menu.lst
```

Get familiar with pacman

pacman is the Arch user's best friend. It is highly recommended to
study and learn how to use the pacman(8) tool. Try:

```
$ man pacman
```

For more information,please look up the pacman wiki entries at
your leisure.

Powerpill, a pacman wrapper script

Before you continue, consider installing Xyne's powerpill (now in
[community]) which is a pacman wrapper script that speeds up
package retrieval by using aria2c (an external download helper) for
concurrent/segmented downloads. In other words, powerpill pulls
packages in parallel effectively speeding up your downloads. This is
particularly advantageous on new installs when pulling down
hundreds of megs of packages.

```
# pacman -S powerpill
```

Treat powerpill as pacman as you consider installations, for
example, the following will update your system:

61

Arch Linux Handbook

```
# powerpill -Syu
```

See the Powerpill wiki article for more.

Step 3: Update System

You are now ready to upgrade your entire system. Before you do, read through the news (and optionally the announce mailing list). Often the developers will provide important information about fixes for known issues. Consulting these pages before any upgrade is good practice.

Sync, refresh, and upgrade your entire new system with:

```
# pacman -Syu
```

you may also use:

```
# pacman --sync --refresh --sysupgrade
```

pacman will now download a fresh copy of the master package list from the server(s) defined in pacman.conf(5) and perform all available upgrades. (You may be prompted to upgrade pacman itself at this point. If so, say yes, and then reissue the pacman -Syu command when finished.)

Reboot if a kernel upgrade has occurred.

> **Note:** Occasionally, configuration changes may take place requiring user action during an update; read pacman's output for any pertinent information.

Pacman output is saved in /var/log/pacman.log.

See Package Management FAQs for answers to frequently asked questions regarding updating and managing your packages.

Part II: Configure&Update the New Arch Linux base
system

The Arch rolling release model

Keep in mind that Arch is a **rolling release** distribution. This means
there is never a reason to reinstall or perform elaborate system
rebuilds to upgrade to the newest version. Simply issuing **pacman
-Syu** periodically keeps your entire system up-to-date and on the
bleeding edge. At the end of this upgrade, your system is
completely current. **Reboot** if a kernel upgrade has occurred.

Network Time Protocol

You may wish to set the system time now using OpenNTPD to sync
the local clock to remote NTP servers. OpenNTPD may also be
added to the DAEMONS= array in /etc/rc.conf to provide this
service at each boot. (See the Network Time Protocol article.)

Step 4: Add a user and setup groups

UNIX is a multi-user environment. You should not do your
everyday work using the root account. It is more than poor practice;
it is dangerous. Root is for administrative tasks. Instead, add a
normal, non-root user account using the /usr/sbin/useradd
program:

```
# useradd -m -G [groups] -s [login_shell] [username]
```

- **-m** Creates user home directory as /home/**username**.
  Within their home directory, a user can write files, delete
  them, install programs, etc. Users' home directories shall
  contain their data and personal configuration files, the so-
  called 'dot files' (their name is preceded by a dot), which
  are 'hidden'. (To view dotfiles, enable the appropriate
  option in your file manager or run ls with the -a switch.) If
  there is a conflict between *user* (under /home/username)
  and *global* configuration files, (usually under /etc/) the
  settings in the *user* file will prevail. Dotfiles likely to be
  altered by the end user include .xinitrc and .bashrc files.
  The configuration files for xinit and Bash respectively.

63

Arch Linux Handbook

They allow the user the ability to change the window manager to be started upon login and also aliases, user-specified commands and environment variables respectively. When a user is created, their dotfiles shall be taken from the /etc/skel directory where system sample files reside.

- **-G** A list of supplementary groups which the user is also a member of. *Each group is separated from the next by a comma, with no intervening spaces.* The default is for the user to belong only to the initial group (users).
- **-s** The path and filename of the user's default login shell.

Useful groups for your non-root user include:

- **audio** - for tasks involving sound card and related software
- **floppy** - for access to a floppy if applicable
- **lp** - for managing printing tasks
- **optical** - for managing tasks pertaining to the optical drive(s)
- **storage** - for managing storage devices
- **video** - for video tasks and 3d acceleration
- **wheel** - for using sudo
- **power** - used w/ power options (ie. shutdown w/ off button)

A typical desktop system example, adding a user named "archie" specifying bash as the login shell:

```
# useradd -m -G
users,audio,lp,optical,storage,video,wheel,power -s
/bin/bash archie
```

Next, add a password for your new user using /usr/bin/passwd.

An example for our user, 'archie':

```
# passwd archie
```

(You will be prompted to provide the new UNIX password.)

64

Part II: Configure&Update the New Arch Linux base system

Your new non-root user has now been created, complete with a home directory and a login password.

Alternative method, using /usr/sbin/adduser:

Alternatively, you may use adduser, an interactive user adding program which will prompt you for the above data: *(recommended for beginners)*

```
# adduser
```

Deleting the user account:

In the event of error, or if you wish to delete this user account in favor of a different name or for any other reason, use /usr/sbin/userdel:

```
# userdel -r [username]
```

- -r Files in the user's home directory will be removed along with the home directory itself and the user's mail spool.

If you want to change the name of your user or any existing user, see the Change username page of the wiki and/or the Groups and User Management articles for further information. You may also check the man pages for usermod(8) and gpasswd(8).

Step 5: Install and setup Sudo (Optional)

To install Sudo:

```
# pacman -S sudo
```

To add a user as a sudo user (a "sudoer"), the visudo command must be run as root. If you do not know how to use vi, you may set the EDITOR environment variable to the editor of your choice before running visudo. e.g.:

65

Arch Linux Handbook

```
# EDITOR=nano visudo
```

If you are comfortable using vi, issue the visudo command without the EDITOR=nano variable:

```
# visudo
```

This will open the file /etc/sudoers in a special session of vi. visudo copies the file to be edited to a temporary file, edits it with an editor, (vi by default), and subsequently runs a sanity check. If it passes, the temporary file overwrites the original with the correct permissions.

> **Warning:** Do not edit /etc/sudoers directly with an editor; Errors in syntax can cause annoyances (like rendering the root account unusable). You must use the *visudo* command to edit /etc/sudoers.

To give the user full root privileges when he/she precedes a command with "sudo", add the following line:

```
USER_NAME    ALL=(ALL) ALL
```

where USER_NAME is the username of the individual.

For more information, such as sudoer <TAB> completion, see Sudo

Part III: Install X and configure ALSA

Step 1: Configure sound with alsamixer

The Advanced Linux Sound Architecture (known by the acronym **ALSA**) is a Linux kernel component intended to replace the original Open Sound System (OSS) for providing device drivers for sound cards. Besides the sound device drivers, **ALSA** also bundles a user space library for application developers who want to use driver features with a higher level API than direct interaction with the kernel drivers.

> **Note:** Alsa is included in the Arch mainline kernel and udev will automatically probe your hardware on boot-up, loading the corresponding kernel module for your audio card. Therefore, your sound should already be working, but upstream sources mute all channels by default.

> **Note:** OSS4.1 has been released under a free license and is generally considered a significant improvement over older OSS versions. If you have issues with ALSA, or simply wish to explore another option, you may choose OSS4.1 instead. Instructions can be found in OSS

The alsa-utils package contains the alsamixer userspace tool, which allows configuration of the sound device from the console or terminal.

By default the upstream kernel sources ship with snd_pcsp, the alsa pc speaker module. snd_pcsp is usually loaded before your "actual" sound card module. In most cases, it will be more convenient if this module is loaded last, as it will allow alsamixer to correctly control the desired sound card.

To have snd_pcsp load last, add the following to /etc/modprobe.d/modprobe.conf:

67

Arch Linux Handbook

```
options snd-pcsp index=2
```

Alternatively, if you do not want snd_pcsp to load at all, blacklist it by adding the following to /etc/rc.conf:

```
MODULES=(... !snd_pcsp)
```

> **Note:** You will need to unload all your sound modules and reload them for the changes to take effect. It might be easier to reboot. Your choice.

Install the alsa-utils package:

```
# pacman -S alsa-utils
```

Also, you may want to install the alsa-oss package, which wraps applications written for OSS in a compatibility library, allowing them to work with ALSA. To install the alsa-oss package:

```
# pacman -S alsa-oss
```

Did you add your normal user to the audio group? If not, use /usr/bin/gpasswd. As root do:

```
# gpasswd -a yourusername audio
```

As **normal, non-root** user, invoke /usr/bin/alsamixer:

```
# su - yourusername
$ alsamixer
```

Unmute the Master and PCM channels by scrolling to them with cursor left/right and pressing **M**. Increase the volume levels with the

68

Part III: Install X and configure ALSA

cursor-up key. (70-90 Should be a safe range.) Some machines, (like the Thinkpad T61), have a **Speaker** channel which must be unmuted and adjusted as well. Leave alsamixer by pressing ESC.

Sound test

Ensure your speakers are properly connected, and test your sound configuration as normal user using **/usr/bin/aplay**:

```
$ aplay /usr/share/sounds/alsa/Front_Center.wav
```

You should hear a very eloquent woman say, "Front, center."

Saving the Sound Settings

Exit your normal user shell and run **/usr/sbin/alsactl** as root:

```
$ exit
# alsactl store
```

This will create the file '/etc/asound.state', saving the alsamixer settings.

Also, add the alsa *daemon* to your DAEMONS section in /etc/rc.conf to automatically restore the mixer settings on boot-up.

```
# nano /etc/rc.conf
DAEMONS=(syslog-ng network crond alsa)
```

Note that the alsa daemon merely restores your volume mixer levels on boot up by reading /etc/asound.state. It is separate from the alsa audio library (and kernel level API).

Expanded information available in the ALSA wiki entry.

69

Arch Linux Handbook

Step 2: Install X

The **X** Window System version 11 (commonly **X11**, or just simply **X**) is a networking and display protocol which provides windowing on bitmap displays. It provides the standard toolkit and protocol to build graphical user interfaces (GUIs) on UNIX-like operating systems.

X provides the basic framework, or primitives, for building GUI environments: drawing and moving windows on the screen and interacting with a mouse and/or keyboard. **X** does not mandate the user interface — individual client programs handle this.

X is so named because it was preceded by the **W** Window System, originally developed at Stanford University.

> **Note:** If you plan on using an **open-source** video driver, and need 3d acceleration, it is recommended to install the libgl library before installing Xorg:

```
# pacman -S libgl
```

(Proprietary video drivers provide their own gl library implementations.)

A: Install X

Now we will install the base Xorg packages using pacman. This is the first step in building a GUI.

```
# pacman -S xorg
```

With newer versions of xorg, it is suggested (and possibly necessary in most cases) to install the input driver evdev, which should be installed as a dependency for xorg-server, but many seem to be lacking somehow:

70

Part III: Install X and configure ALSA

```
# pacman -S xf86-input-evdev
```

The 3d utilities glxgears and glxinfo are included in the **mesa** package:

```
# pacman -S mesa
```

B: Install Video Driver Package

Now we have the base packages we need for running the **X** Server. You should add the driver for your graphics card now (e.g. xf86-video-<name>). The easiest way to configure X.org is by installing the correct driver packages first, and then generating /etc/X11/xorg.conf using an autoconfiguration script, like Xorg -configure.

You will need knowledge of which video chipset your machine has. If you do not know, use the `/usr/sbin/lspci` program:

```
# lspci | grep VGA
```

If you need a list of all **open-source** video drivers, do:

```
# pacman -Ss xf86-video | less
```

Here is a list of **open source** drivers, and the corresponding video chipsets.

- **xf86-video-apm** — Alliance ProMotion video driver
- **xf86-video-ark** — ark video driver
- **xf86-video-ati** — ATI(AMD) video driver
    - **xf86-video-r128** — ATI(AMD) video driver for X.org ati Rage128 video
    - **xf86-video-mach64** — ATI(AMD) video driver for X.org mach64 video

71

Arch Linux Handbook

- **xf86-video-radeonhd** — open source radeonhd driver
- **xf86-video-chips** — Chips and Technologies video driver
- **xf86-video-cirrus** — Cirrus Logic video driver
- **xf86-video-dummy** — dummy video driver
- **xf86-video-fbdev** — framebuffer video driver
- **xf86-video-glint** — GLINT/Permedia video driver
- **xf86-video-i128** — Number 0 i128 video driver
- **xf86-video-i740** — Intel i740 video driver
- **xf86-video-i810** — Intel i810/i830/i9xx video drivers (deprecated - use -intel)
- **xf86-video-intel** — Newer Version of Intel i810/i830/i9xx video drivers
- **xf86-video-intel-legacy** — Legacy-driver for older intel cards as 82865G (xf86-video-intel currently crashes with older cards)
- **xf86-video-imstt** — Integrated Micro Solutions Twin Turbo video driver
- **xf86-video-mga** — mga video driver (Matrox Graphics Adapter)
- **xf86-video-neomagic** — neomagic video driver
- **xf86-video-nv** — Nvidia nv video driver
- **xf86-video-nouveau** — Open Source 3D acceleration driver for nVidia cards (experimental), check: [1] for Current Status
- **xf86-video-openchrome** — VIA/S3G UniChrome, UniChrome Pro and Chrome9 video driver
- **xf86-video-rendition** — Rendition video driver
- **xf86-video-s3** — S3 video driver
- **xf86-video-s3virge** — S3 Virge video driver
- **xf86-video-savage** — savage video driver
- **xf86-video-siliconmotion** — siliconmotion video driver
- **xf86-video-sis** — SiS video driver
- **xf86-video-sisusb** — SiS USB video driver
- **xf86-video-tdfx** — tdfx video driver
- **xf86-video-trident** — Trident video driver
- **xf86-video-tseng** — tseng video driver

Part III: Install X and configure ALSA

- **xf86-video-unichrome** — VIA S3 Unichrome video drivers
- **xf86-video-v4l** — v4l video driver
- **xf86-video-vesa** — vesa video driver
- **xf86-video-vga** — VGA 16 color video driver
- **xf86-video-vmware** — vmware video driver
- **xf86-video-voodoo** — voodoo video driver

Note: The **vesa** driver is the most generic, and should work with almost any modern video chipset. If you cannot find a suitable driver for your video chipset, vesa *should* work.

Use pacman to install the appropriate video driver for your video card/onboard video. e.g.:

```
# pacman -S xf86-video-savage
```

(for the Savage driver.)

- If you have an NVIDIA or ATI graphics card you may wish to install the proprietary NVIDIA or ATI drivers. **Installing proprietary video drivers is covered below.**.
- If you do not want to install the proprietary drivers or do not have an NVIDIA or ATI graphics card, you should skip down to **Step 3: Configure X**.

NVIDIA Graphics Cards

The NVIDIA proprietary drivers are generally considered to be of good quality, and offer 3D performance, whereas the open source **nv** driver offers only 2d support at this time.

Before you configure your Graphics Card you will need to know which driver fits. Arch currently has several different driver packages that each match a certain subset of Cards:

1. nvidia-96xx *slightly newer cards up to the GF 4.*

2. nvidia-173xx *Geforce FX series cards*

3. nvidia *newest GPUs after the GF FX*

73

Arch Linux Handbook

> **Note:** Nvidia-71xx series proprietary drivers, which are required by extremely old cards like TNT and TNT2, have been removed because they do not work with the new Xorg that Arch makes use of and nvidia has discontinued support for such. You should use the xf86-video-nv or xf86-video-vesa drivers instead.

Consult the NVIDIA website to see which one is for you. The difference is only for the installation; Configuration works the same with every driver.

Select and install the appropriate NVIDIA driver *for your card*, e.g.:

```
# pacman -S nvidia-96xx
```

The NVIDIA package has a utility for updating your existing /etc/X11/xorg.conf for use with the NVIDIA driver:

```
# nvidia-xconfig
```

It also has several options which will further specify the contents and options of the xorg.conf file. For example,

```
# nvidia-xconfig --composite --add-argb-glx-visuals
```

For more detailed information, see nvidia-xconfig(1).

Some useful tweaking options in the device section are (beware that these may not work on your system):

```
Option          "RenderAccel" "true"
Option          "NoLogo" "true"
Option          "AGPFastWrite" "true"
Option          "EnablePageFlip" "true"
```

Make sure all instances of DRI are commented out:

Part III: Install X and configure ALSA

```
#     Load      "dri"
```

Double check your /etc/X11/xorg.conf to make sure your default depth, horizontal sync, vertical refresh, and resolutions are acceptable.

Update kernel module dependencies using /sbin/depmod:

```
# depmod -a
```

(A reboot may be necessary.)

> **Tip:** Advanced instructions for NVIDIA configuration can be found in the NVIDIA article.

You may now continue with **Step 3: Configure X** to familiarize yourself further, or continue the installation process with **Test X**.

ATI Graphics Cards

ATI owners have multiple options for drivers.

- The open source *radeon* driver provided by the **xf86-video-ati** package.
  - This is the original, reverse-engineered open source driver which fully supports Radeon chipsets up to X1950 (latest R500 chipsets). Cards up to the 9200 series are fully supported, stable, and provide full 2D and 3D acceleration. Cards from 9500 to X1950 feature full 2D acceleration, and good 3D acceleration, but lack certain features provided by the proprietary driver, (for example, powersaving is still in a testing phase). Cards from HD2xxx (R6xx) to the newest are supported by xf86-video-ati, but only offer 2d support at this time.
- The open source *radeonhd* driver provided by the **xf86-video-radeonhd** package.

Arch Linux Handbook

- This driver supports ATI R500 chipsets (Radeon X1000 series) and newer. It is written by Novell with specifications provided to the public by AMD. It supports RandR 1.2 and development is currently very active. Therefore, functionality may be inconsistent across the spectrum of cards supported. (Some users report excellent performance and reliability while others experience trouble.) It also supports HDMI, with sound.
- The proprietary *fglrx* driver provided by the Catalyst package located in the AUR. The proprietary driver is covered below.

The open-source drivers will usually suit most needs along with being generally less problematic.

Install the *radeon* ATI Driver with

```
# pacman -S xf86-video-ati libgl ati-dri
```

Install the *radeonhd* ATi Driver with

```
# pacman -S xf86-video-radeonhd libgl ati-dri
```

The proprietary ATI driver **Catalyst** was once a precompiled package offered by Arch in the extra repository, but as of March 2009, official support has been dropped because of dissatisfaction with the quality and speed of development of the proprietary driver.The catalyst driver is now available in AUR. Installation information for Catalyst driver is available here

> **Warning:** The proprietary ATI driver supports only R600 and newer devices (that means, HD2xxx and newer). The older ones (X1xxx and older) aren't supported.

> **Tip:** Advanced instructions for ATI configuration can be found in the ATI wiki article.

Part III: Install X and configure ALSA

C: Install Input Driver Packages

The latest X requires you to install drivers for your input devices,
keyboard and mouse included. For a complete list of available input
drivers,

```
# pacman -Ss xf86-input | less
```

For most users, xf86-input-keyboard and xf86-input-mouse should
be sufficient for a basic setup. Use pacman to install your desired
drivers for your input devices. e.g.:

```
# pacman -S xf86-input-keyboard
```

Step 3: Configure X

A: The xorg.conf file

/etc/X11/xorg.conf is the main configuration file for your **X**
Window System, the foundation of your **G**raphical **U**ser **I**nterface.
It is a plain text file ordered into sections and subsections. Important
sections are *Files, InputDevice, Module, Monitor, Modes, Screen,
Device, and ServerLayout.* Sections can appear in any order and
there may be more than one section of each kind, for example, if
you have more than one monitor, or if your laptop has a trackpoint
as well as a mouse.

Since X11R7.2 the X.Org X Server features autoconfiguration.
Therefore, it can function without an xorg.conf file in many cases.
If the autoconfiguration *works satisfactorily* and you do not need to
specify special features such as aiglx, compositing and so forth, you
may forgo creating an xorg.conf file.

77

Arch Linux Handbook

Standard xorg.conf generation

Advanced users may wish to manually create their own xorg.conf file. You may also use the /usr/bin/Xorg program with the -configure option to generate a basic config file; As root, do:

```
# Xorg -configure
```

This will create a config file at /root/xorg.conf.new

Copy the file to /etc/X11/:

```
# cp /root/xorg.conf.new /etc/X11/xorg.conf
```

Alternative xorg.conf generation

Newer versions of the Xorg Server(>1.6) do not include the /usr/bin/xorgconfig or /usr/bin/xorgcfg scripts. If you run into problems generating/using an xorg.conf file, you might want to consider using this guide.

See the article on X.Org, section "Without xorg.conf".

- Note that if you are in possession of a properly configured xorg.conf under another distribution and with the same Xorg version, you may easily copy it over to your current Arch system's /etc/X11/ directory.

B: Input hotplugging

Input hotplugging is supported since the 1.4 version of the X.Org X Server and enabled by default. When enabled, X will utilize hal to allow for the hotplugging and removal of human interface devices without having to restart X.

Part III: Install X and configure ALSA

Warning: Starting the **X** server using input hotplugging without the **HAL** daemon installed and running may result in the inability to use the mouse and/or keyboard, and the **X** server appearing to freeze as a result .

You must decide whether you will use input hotplugging (enabled by default), or disable it. Input hotplugging is convenient for many users, especially those with mobile machines like laptops and netbooks. Other users may wish to disable it in favor of manual or more static device configuration within /etc/xorg.conf.

Tip: See the article on Xorg input hotplugging for full details.

Using input hotplugging

Install HAL, dbus and the evdev input driver:

```
# pacman -S hal dbus xf86-input-evdev
```

Set the keyboard layout (if you do not use a standard US keyboard)

```
# cp /usr/share/hal/fdi/policy/10osvendor/10-
keymap.fdi /etc/hal/fdi/policy/
# nano /etc/hal/fdi/policy/10-keymap.fdi
```

Edit the "input.xkb.layout" key and possibly the "input.xkb.variant" key in this file.

Laptop users will also need the synaptics package to allow X to configure the touchpad:

Arch Linux Handbook

```
# pacman -S xf86-input-synaptics
```

Tip: For instructions on fine tuning or troubleshooting touchpad settings, see the Touchpad Synaptics article.

The HAL daemon

The hal daemon **must** be started **before** the **X** server:

```
# /etc/rc.d/hal start
```

Add the hal daemon to the DAEMONS array in /etc/rc.conf to start it at every boot.

Disable input hotplugging

Disabling input hotplugging will skip devices detected by hal and will use the keyboard/mouse configuration from xorg.conf:

```
# nano /etc/X11/xorg.conf
```

add the following:

```
Section "ServerFlags"
    Option "AutoAddDevices" "False"
EndSection
```

Set the keyboard layout if not using a standard US keyboard

Add option lines in the "InputDevice" section of the /etc/X11/xorg.conf file specifying the keyboard layout and variant:

80

Part III: Install X and configure ALSA

```
Option "XkbLayout" "be"
Option "XkbVariant" ""
```

Alternative method using the setxkbmap command:

```
# setxkbmap pl
```

(with the proper keyboard layout instead of pl of course) should switch your keyboard layout in x. To make this permanent, add this command to /home/<youruser>/.xinitrc before starting the window manager (before command like exec startxfce4).

C: Test X

First, read the warning about input hotplugging in the previous section. To test the X server, run the **X** script with the *-config* flag against the *path/to/xorg.conf* file. e.g.:

```
# X -config /etc/X11/xorg.conf
```

X should start with the white hollow vector **X** in the center of the screen, which should respond to mouse, trackpoint or touchpad movement. Use CTRL-Alt-Backspace to exit **X**.

> **Note:** Some users have found after the upgrade to Xorg 1.6 that this test fails (no hollow X appears and no capacity for cursor movement is enabled), but this does not indicate a problem with the installation of X. You may want to double check by running the next test in this guide.

81

Arch Linux Handbook

> **Note:** With Xorg 1.6 CTRL-Alt-Backspace has been deprecated and will not work to exit out of this test. A somewhat messy work around is to switch to a different virtual console (CTRL-Alt-F2, for example) and then switch back to the console the test is running in (probably CTRL-Alt-F1). You will then be able to use CTRL-C to kill the X test. You can enable CTRL-Alt-Backspace by editing xorg.conf, as described here.

In case of errors

Inspect the config file:

```
# nano /etc/X11/xorg.conf
```

Ensure the video driver is properly specified. e.g.:

```
Section "Device"

        ...

        Driver   "savage"

        ...

EndSection
```

Ensure there are horizontal sync and vertical refresh specs under section "Monitor". If not, add them:

Part III: Install X and configure ALSA

```
Section "Monitor"
        Identifier    "Monitor0"
        VendorName    "Monitor Vendor"
        ModelName     "Monitor Model"
        HorizSync     30.0 - 130.0 # Safe for LCD's
        VertRefresh   50.0 - 100.0 # Safe for LCD's and
most CRT's.
EndSection
```

(If these specs are unknown, consult the documentation of the computer monitor.)

Specify your default color depth under section "Screen":

```
Section "Screen"
        Identifier "Screen0"
        Device     "Card0"
        Monitor    "Monitor0"
        DefaultDepth 24
```

(Typically, this will be set to 24 for true color.)

Also add your desired Modes to your "Display" subsection, at least under the Depth 24 header, e.g.:

```
SubSection "Display"
                Viewport   0 0
                Depth      24
                Modes "1024x768" "800x600" "640x480"
```

Add the following section, if eye candy which requires the composite extension is desired:

```
Section "Extensions"
        Option "Composite" "Enable"
EndSection
```

Try the config again, after modifying:

83

Arch Linux Handbook

```
# X -config /etc/X11/xorg.conf
```

Detailed instructions in the Xorg article.

- **Using wgetpaste**

If you are still having trouble after consulting the Xorg article and need assistance via the Arch forums, be sure to install and use wgetpaste:

```
# pacman -S wgetpaste
```

Use wgetpaste and provide links for the following files when asking for help in your forum post:

- ~/.xinitrc
- /etc/X11/xorg.conf
- /var/log/Xorg.0.log.old

Use wgetpaste like so:

```
$ wgetpaste </path/to/file>
```

Post the corresponding links given within your forum post. Be sure to provide appropriate hardware and driver information as well.

Simple baseline X test(if necessary)

At this point, you should have xorg installed, with a suitable video driver and an /etc/X11/xorg.conf configuration file. If you want to test your configuration quickly, to ensure your ability to successfully start **X** from the command line before installing a complete desktop environment, you can do so by configuring ~/.xinitrc to invoke **Xterm**. Xterm is a very simple terminal emulator which runs in the **X** Server environment; it is installed as part of the base xorg packages. More advanced users who are comfortable with **X** configuration may choose to skip this optional step.

84

Part III: Install X and configure ALSA

Prepare for the test by configuring ~/.xinitrc

One of the main functions of this file is to dictate what **X** Window client is invoked with the **/usr/bin/startx** and/or **/usr/bin/xinit** program *on a per-user basis.* (The **startx** script is merely a front end to the more versatile **xinit** command.) There are vast amounts of additional configurable specifications and commands that may also be added to ~/.xinitrc as you further customize your system.

> **Note: .xinitrc** is a so-called 'dot' (.) file. Files in a UNIX filesystem which are preceded with a dot (.) are 'hidden', and will not show up with a regular 'ls' command, usually for the sake of keeping directories tidy. Dot files may be seen by issuing **ls -a**. The 'rc' denotes *Run Commands* and simply indicates that it is a configuration file. Since it controls how a program runs, it is (although historically incorrect) also said to stand for "Run Control".

startx/xinit will start the **X** server and clients. To determine the client to run, **startx/xinit** will first look to parse a .xinitrc file in the user's home directory. In the absence of file ~/.xinitrc, it defaults to the global xinitrc in the xinit library directory; /etc/X11/xinit/xinitrc, which defaults to using the TWM window manager. (Hence, if you invoke startx without a ~/.xinitrc file, a TWM session will start.) Further details in the .xinitrc wiki entry.

Switch to your *normal, non-root* user:

```
# su - yourusername
```

- /etc/skel/ contains files and directories to provide sane defaults for newly created user accounts. The name **skel** is derived from the word **skeleton**, because the files it contains form the basic structure for users' home directories.
- If you installed from a fresh (Core) install, it does not include the X window manager, so .xinitrc does not exist in /etc/skel. Instead, use the sample provided here (If you've

85

Arch Linux Handbook

> followed the guide step by step you should have a basic .xinitrc file in /etc/skel).

Copy the sample xinitrc file from /etc/skel/ to your home directory:

```
$ cp /etc/skel/.xinitrc ~/
```

Edit the file:

```
$ nano ~/.xinitrc
```

and add "exec xterm" so that it looks like this:

```
#!/bin/sh
#
# ~/.xinitrc
#
# Executed by startx (run your window manager from here)
#
# exec wmaker
# exec startkde
# exec icewm
# exec blackbox
# exec fluxbox
#
exec xterm
```

> **Note:** *Be sure to have only **one** uncommented **exec** line in your ~/.xinitrc.*

Below, we shall edit this file again to specify the appropriate desktop environment/window manager of your choice.

Perform the test

Test your configurations by starting **X** as **normal, non-root** user, with:

Part III: Install X and configure ALSA

```
$ startx
```

or

```
$ xinit
```

You should have an **xterm** session open up. You can test your keyboard and its layout in it. You may have to move your mouse around until it enters the xterm area before you see the mouse cursor or xterm responds to your keyboard.

You can exit the **X** Server with Ctrl+Alt+Backspace, or by typing "exit". If you have problems starting **X**, you can look for errors in the /var/log/Xorg.0.log file and on the console output of the console you started **X** from.

If you prove a properly configured /etc/X11/xorg.conf by successfully running the test, you can be assured that your DE/WM of choice will work smoothly.

> **Tip:** Advanced instructions for Xorg configuration can be found in the Xorg article.

Part IV: Installing and configuring a Desktop Environment

Part IV: Installing and configuring a Desktop Environment

While The **X** Window System provides the basic framework for building a *graphical user interface* (GUI), a **Desktop Environment** (DE), works atop and in conjunction with **X**, to provide a completely functional and dynamic GUI. A DE typically provides a window manager, icons, applets, windows, toolbars, folders, wallpapers, a suite of applications and abilities like drag and drop. The particular functionalities and designs of each DE will uniquely affect your overall environment and experience. Therefore, choosing a DE is a very subjective and personal decision. Choose the best environment for *your* needs.

- If you want something full-featured and similar to Windows and Mac OSX, **KDE** is a good choice
- If you want something slightly more minimalist, which follows the K.I.S.S. principle more closely, **GNOME** is a good choice
- **Xfce** is generally perceived as similar to GNOME, but lighter and less demanding on system resources, yet still visually pleasing and providing a very complete environment.
- **LXDE** is a minimal DE based on the Openbox window manager. It provides most things you need for a modern desktop while keeping relatively low system resource usage. LXDE is a good choice for those who want a quick way of setting up a pre-configured Openbox system.

If you desire a lighter, less demanding GUI to configure manually, you may choose to simply install a **Window Manager**, or WM. A WM controls the placement and appearance of application windows in conjunction with the X Window System but does NOT include such features as panels, applets, icons, applications, etc., by default.

- Lightweight floating WM's include: **Openbox, Fluxbox, fvwm2, pekwm, evilwm, Windowmaker, and TWM**.

Arch Linux Handbook

- If you need something completely different, try a tiling WM like **awesome, ion3, wmii, dwm, xmonad,** or **ratpoison.**

Step 1: Install Fonts

At this point, you may wish to save time by installing visually pleasing, true type fonts, before installing a desktop environment/window manager. Dejavu and bitstream-vera are good, general-purpose font sets. You may also want to have the Microsoft font sets, which are especially popular on websites.

Install with:

```
# pacman -S ttf-ms-fonts ttf-dejavu ttf-bitstream-vera
```

Step 2: ~/.xinitrc (again)

As **non-root user**, edit your /home/username/.xinitrc to specify the DE you wish to use. This will allow you to use **startx/xinit** from the shell, in the future, to open your DE/WM of choice:

```
$ nano ~/.xinitrc
```

Uncomment or add the '**exec ..**' line of the appropriate desktop environment/window manager. Some examples are below:

For the Xfce4 desktop environment:

```
exec startxfce4
```

For the KDE desktop environment:

90

Part IV: Installing and configuring a Desktop Environment

```
exec startkde
```

A **startkde** or **startxfce4** command starts the KDE or Xfce4
desktop environment. This command does not finish until you
logout of the DE. Normally the shell would wait for KDE to finish,
then run the next command. The "exec" prefix to this command tells
the shell that this is the last command, so the shell does not need to
wait to run a subsequent command.

If you have trouble with automounting, use the following command
instead. Replace "startxfce4" with the command that is appropriate
for your window manager.

```
exec ck-launch-session startxfce4
```

Remember to have only one uncommented **exec** line in your
~/.xinitrc.

Step 3: Install a Desktop Environment

Continue below, installing the DE/WM of your choice.

- **GNOME**
- **KDE**
- **Xfce**
- **LXDE**
- **Openbox**
- **Fluxbox**
- **fvwm2**

GNOME

About GNOME

The **G**NU **N**etwork **O**bject **M**odel **E**nvironment. The GNOME
project provides two things: The GNOME desktop environment, an
intuitive and attractive desktop for end-users, and the GNOME

91

Arch Linux Handbook

development platform, an extensive framework for building applications that integrate into the rest of the desktop.

Installation

Install the base GNOME environment with:

```
# pacman -S gnome
```

Additionally, you can install the extras:

```
# pacman -S gnome-extra
```

It's safe to choose all packages shown in the extra package.

Useful DAEMONS for GNOME

Recall from above that a daemon is a program that runs in the background, waiting for events to occur and offering services. Some users prefer to use the **hal** daemon. The **hal** daemon, among other things, will automate the mounting of disks, optical drives, and USB drives/thumbdrives for use in the GUI. The **fam** daemon will allow real-time representation of file alterations in the GUI, allowing instant access to recently installed programs, or changes in the file system. Both **hal** and **fam** can make life easier for the GNOME user. The hal and fam packages are installed when you install GNOME, but must be invoked to become useful.

You may want to install a graphical login manager. For GNOME, the **gdm** daemon is a good choice.

As root:

```
# pacman -S gdm
```

Start hal and fam:

92

Part IV: Installing and configuring a Desktop Environment

```
# /etc/rc.d/hal start

# /etc/rc.d/fam start
```

Add them to your /etc/rc.conf DAEMONS section, so they will be invoked at boot:

```
# nano /etc/rc.conf

DAEMONS=(syslog-ng network crond alsa hal fam gdm)
```

(If you prefer to log into the console and manually start X, leave out gdm.)

Then edit your /etc/gdm/custom.conf and in the **[servers]** section add:

```
0=Standard vt7
```

As normal user, start X:

```
$ startx
```

or

```
$ xinit
```

If ~/.xinitrc is not configured for GNOME, you may always start it with **xinit**, followed by the path to GNOME:

93

Arch Linux Handbook

```
$ xinit /usr/bin/gnome-session
```

Tip: Advanced instructions for installing and configuring GNOME can be found in the Gnome article.

Congratulations! Welcome to your GNOME desktop environment on your new Arch Linux system! You may wish to continue by viewing **Tweaks and finishing touches,** or the rest of the information below. You may also be interested in the Post Installation Tips wiki article.

Eye Candy

By default, GNOME does not come with many themes and icons. You may wish to install some more attractive artwork for GNOME:

A nice gtk (gui widget) theme engine (includes themes) is the murrine engine. Install with:

```
# pacman -S gtk-engine-murrine
```

Optional for more themes:

```
# pacman -S murrine-themes-collection
```

Once it has been installed, select it with System -> Preferences -> Appearance -> Theme tab.

The Arch Linux repositories also have a few more nice themes and engines. Install the following to see for yourself:

```
# pacman -S gtk-engines gtk-aurora-engine gtk-candido-
engine gtk-rezlooks-engine
```

You can find many more themes, icons, and wallpapers at GNOME-Look.

94

Part IV: Installing and configuring a Desktop Environment

KDE

About KDE

The **K D**esktop **E**nvironment. KDE is a powerful Free Software graphical desktop environment for GNU/Linux and UNIX workstations. It combines ease of use, contemporary functionality, and outstanding graphical design with the technological superiority of UNIX-like operating systems.

Installation

Choose one of the following, then continue below with **Useful KDE DAEMONS**:

1. The package **kde** is the official and complete vanilla KDE 4.2 residing under the Arch [extra] repo.

Install base kde:

```
# pacman -S kdebase-workspace
```

Install the whole Desktop Environment:

```
# pacman -S kde
```

or

```
# pacman -S kde-meta
```

2. Alternatively, there exists a project called **KDEmod** (recently referred to collectively as the Chakra project). It is an Arch Linux exclusive, community-driven system, designed for modularity and offers a choice between KDE 3.5.10 or 4.x.x. KDEmod can be installed with pacman, after adding the proper repository to /etc/pacman.conf. The project website, including complete installation instructions, can be found at http://www.chakra-project.org/.

95

Arch Linux Handbook

Useful KDE DAEMONS

Recall from above that a daemon is a program that runs in the background, waiting for events to occur and offering services.

KDE will require the **hal** (**H**ardware **A**bstraction **L**ayer) daemon for optimal functionality. The hal daemon, among other things, will facilitate the automatic mounting of disks, optical drives, and USB drives/thumbdrives for use in the GUI. The hal package is installed when you install xorg-server, but must be invoked to become useful.

The **kdm** daemon is the **K D**isplay **M**anager, which provides a **graphical login**, if desired.

Start hal:

```
# /etc/rc.d/hal start
```

Note: The hal daemon relies on, and will automatically start, the dbus daemon.

Edit your DAEMONS array in /etc/rc.conf:

```
# nano /etc/rc.conf
```

Add **hal** to your DAEMONS array, to invoke it on boot. If you prefer a graphical login, add **kdm** as well:

```
DAEMONS=(syslog-ng hal network crond alsa kdm)
```

Note: If you installed KDEmod3 instead of normal KDE, use kdm3 instead of kdm.

Part IV: Installing and configuring a Desktop Environment

- This method will start the system at runlevel 3, (/etc/inittab default, multiuser mode), and then start KDM as a daemon.

- Some users prefer an alternative method of starting a display manager like KDM on boot by utilizing the /etc/inittab method and starting the system at runlevel 5. See Adding a login manager (KDM, GDM, or XDM) to automatically boot on startup for more.

- If you prefer to log into the **console** at runlevel 3, and manually start X, leave out kdm, or comment it out with a bang, (!).

Now try starting your X Server as normal user:

```
$ startx
```

or

```
$ xinit
```

Tip: Advanced instructions for installing and configuring KDE can be found in the KDE article.

Congratulations! Welcome to your KDE desktop environment on your new Arch Linux system! You may wish to continue by viewing **The Beginners Guide Appendix**, or the rest of the information below. You may also be interested in the Post Installation Tips wiki article.

Xfce

About Xfce

The cholesterol-free **X** environment. Xfce, like GNOME or KDE, is a desktop environment, but aims to be fast and lightweight while remaining visually appealing and easy to use. It contains a suite of

Arch Linux Handbook

apps like a root window app, window manager, file manager, panel, etc. Xfce is written using the GTK2 toolkit (like GNOME) and contains its own development environment (libraries, daemons, etc) similar to other big DEs. Unlike GNOME or KDE, Xfce is lightweight and designed more around CDE than Windows or Mac. It has a much slower development cycle, but is very stable and fast. Xfce is great for older hardware, and will perform excellently on newer machines as well.

Installation

Install Xfce:

```
# pacman -S xfce4
```

You may also wish to install themes and extras:

```
# pacman -S xfce4-goodies gtk2-themes-collection
```

Note: **xfce4-xfapplet-plugin** (a plugin that allows the use of GNOME applets in the Xfce4 panel) is part of the **xfce4-goodies** group and depends on **gnome-panel**, which in turn depends on **gnome-desktop**. You may wish to take this into consideration before installing, since it represents a significant number of extra dependencies.

If you get errors about dbus-launch then you need to install dbus aswell:

```
# pacman -S dbus
```

If you wish to admire 'Tips and Tricks' on login, install the **fortune-mod** package:

Part IV: Installing and configuring a Desktop Environment

```
# pacman -S fortune-mod
```

Useful DAEMONS

Recall from above that a daemon is a program that runs in the background, waiting for events to occur and offering services. Some Xfce users prefer to use the **hal** daemon. The hal daemon, among other things, will automate the mounting of disks, optical drives, and USB drives/thumbdrives for use in the GUI. The fam daemon will allow real-time representation of file alterations in the GUI, allowing instant access to recently installed programs, or changes in the file system. The hal and fam packages are installed when you install Xfce, but must be invoked to become useful.

Start hal and fam:

```
# /etc/rc.d/hal start

# /etc/rc.d/fam start
```

Note: The hal daemon relies on, and will automatically start, the dbus daemon.

Edit your DAEMONS array in /etc/rc.conf:

```
# nano /etc/rc.conf
```

Add **hal** and **fam** to your DAEMONS array, to invoke them at boot.

Tip: Advanced instructions for installing and configuring Xfce can be found in the Xfce article.

If you wish to install one, see Adding a login manager (KDM, GDM, or XDM) to automatically boot on startup. Otherwise you can login in via the console and run:

99

Arch Linux Handbook

```
$ startxfce4
```

Congratulations! Welcome to your Xfce desktop environment on your new Arch Linux system! You may also be interested in the Post Installation Tips wiki article.

LXDE

About LXDE

LXDE, (for *L*ightweight *X*11 *D*esktop *E*nvironment), is a new project focused on providing a modern desktop environment which aims to be lightweight, fast, intuitive and functional while keeping system resource usage low. LXDE is quite different from other desktop environments, since each component of LXDE is a discrete and independent application, and each can be easily substituted by other programs. This modular design eliminates all unnecessary dependencies and provides more flexibility. Details and screenshots available at: http://lxde.org/

LXDE provides:

1. The OpenBox windowmanager
2. PCManFM File manager
3. LXpanel system panel
4. LXSession session manager
5. LXAppearance GTK+ theme switcher
6. GPicView image viewer
7. Leafpad simple text editor
8. XArchiver: Lightweight, fast, and desktop-independent gtk+-based file archiver
9. LXNM (still under development): Lightweight network manager for LXDE supporting wireless connections

These lightweight and versatile tools combine for quick setup, modularity and simplicity.

Install LXDE with:

100

Part IV: Installing and configuring a Desktop Environment

```
# pacman -S lxde
```

Add:

```
exec startlxde
```

- If you plan on running **nm-applet**, the following command should be used instead

```
exec ck-launch-session startlxde
```

to your ~/.xinitrc and start with *startx* or *xinit*

Tip: Further information available at the LXDE wiki article.

*box

Fluxbox

Fluxbox © is yet another windowmanager for X. It's based on the Blackbox 0.61.1 code. Fluxbox looks like blackbox and handles styles, colors, window placement and similar things exactly like blackbox (100% theme/style compability).

Install Fluxbox using

```
# pacman -S fluxbox fluxconf
```

If you use gdm/kdm a new fluxbox session will be automatically added. Otherwise, you should modify your user's .xinitrc and add this to it:

Arch Linux Handbook

```
exec startfluxbox
```

More information is available in the Fluxbox article.

Openbox

Openbox is a standards compliant, fast, light-weight, extensible window manager.

Openbox works with your applications, and makes your desktop easier to manage. This is because the approach to its development was the opposite of what seems to be the general case for window managers. Openbox was written first to comply with standards and to work properly. Only when that was in place did the team turn to the visual interface.

Openbox is fully functional as a stand-alone working environment, or can be used as a drop-in replacement for the default window manager in the GNOME or KDE desktop environments.

Install openbox using

```
# pacman -S openbox
```

Additional configuration tools are also available, if desired:

```
# pacman -S obconf obmenu
```

Once openbox is installed you will get a message to move menu.xml & rc.xml to ~/.config/openbox/ in your home directory:

Part IV: Installing and configuring a Desktop Environment

```
# su - yourusername
$ mkdir -p ~/.config/openbox/
$ cp /etc/xdg/openbox/rc.xml ~/.config/openbox/
$ cp /etc/xdg/openbox/menu.xml ~/.config/openbox/
```

rc.xml is the main configuration file for OpenBox. It may be manually edited, (or you can use OBconf). **menu.xml** configures the right-click menu.

You may log into OpenBox via graphical login using KDM/GDM, or from the shell using **startx**, in which case you will need to edit your ~/.xinitrc (as non-root user) and add the following:

```
exec openbox-session
```

NOTE: If you plan on running dbus (which is required by hal) then make sure your ~/.xinitrc reads:

```
exec dbus-launch --exit-with-session openbox-session
```

You may also start OpenBox from the shell using **xinit**:

```
$ xinit /usr/bin/openbox-session
```

- Openbox may also be used as the window manager for GNOME, KDE, and Xfce.

For KDM there is nothing left to do; openbox is listed in the sessions menu in KDM.

Some useful, lightweight programs for OpenBox are:

- PyPanel, Tint2, or LXpanel if you want a panel
- feh if you want to set the background
- ROX if you want a simple file manager (also provides simple icons)
- PcmanFM a lightweight but versatile file manager (also provides desktop icon functionality)

103

Arch Linux Handbook

- iDesk (available in AUR) for providing desktop icons
- Graveman for burning CD's or DVD's

Tip: More information is available in the Openbox article.

fvwm2

FVWM is an extremely powerful ICCCM-compliant multiple
virtual desktop window manager for the X Window system.
Development is active, and support is excellent.

Install fvwm2 with

```
# pacman -S fvwm
```

fvwm will automatically be listed in kdm/gdm in the sessions menu.
Otherwise, add

```
exec fvwm
```

to your user's .xinitrc.

Useful Applications

Useful Applications

This page will never be complete. It just shows some good applications for the everyday user.
It might also be worthwhile to check out Lightweight Software as well.

Web browser

Firefox

The ever-popular Firefox web browser is available through pacman, although it does not have its official branding. Therefore, the program appears as its development codename, *Shiretoko*, when opened.

Install with:

```
pacman -S firefox
```

Plugins

Be sure and install 'flashplugin',and the 'mplayer-plugin'packages for a complete web experience:

```
pacman -S flashplugin mplayer-plugin
```

Gecko Media Player

A good replacement of the now ageing *mplayer-plugin*, is Gecko Media Player. More stable combined with MPlayer 1.0RC2. *(No more crashes with Apple Trailers.)*

105

Arch Linux Handbook

```
pacman -S gecko-mediaplayer
```

(Note! Be sure to remove mplayer-plugin if it is already installed.)

Thunderbird is useful for managing your emails. If you are using GNOME you may want to take a look at Epiphany and Evolution; if you are using KDE Konqueror and KMail could be your choice. If you want something completely different you can still use Opera. Finally, if you are working on the system console - or in a terminal session - you could use various text-based browsers like ELinks, Links and Lynx, and manage your emails with Mutt. Pidgin (previously known as Gaim) and Kopete are good instant messengers for GNOME and KDE, respectively. PSI and Gajim are perfect if you are using only Jabber or Google Talk.

Office

A full set of LaTeX Programs: tetex has been popular for many years and still works, and its successor Texlive is available from the extra repository.

KOffice is a revolutionary office suite. It is sharply developing to koffice2.

OpenOffice.org is a complete office suite (similar to Microsoft Office). Abiword is a good, small alternative word processor, and Gnumeric an Excel replacement for the GNOME desktop. Go-openoffice

GIMP (or GIMPShop) is a pixel-based graphics program (similar to Adobe Photoshop), while Inkscape is a vector-based graphics program (like Adobe Illustrator).

Video Player

VLC

VLC Player is a versatile multimedia player which can many different formats, from a disc or file. It also provides the ability to

Useful Applications

stream multimedia over a lan. To install it, simply type the code below.

```
pacman -S vlc
```

Mplayer

MPlayer is a multimedia player for Linux. To install it, simply type the code below.

```
pacman -S mplayer
```

It also has a Mozilla plug-in for videos and streams embedded in web pages. To install it, simply type the code below. **NOTE**: mplayer-plugin is considered to be obsolete, please see Gecko Media Player above.

```
pacman -S mplayer-plugin
```

If you use KDE, KMplayer is a better choice. It comes with a plug-in for videos and streams embedded in web pages, which works with Konqueror. To install it, simply type the code below.

```
pacman -S kmplayer
```

Xine

Xine is an excellent player, especially for DVDs.

107

Arch Linux Handbook

```
pacman -S xine-ui
```

libdvdcss

The libdvdcss library provides DVD decoding for encrypted DVDs.
*Ensure the legality of using libdvdcss in your country before
installing!*

```
pacman -S libdvdcss
```

Totem

Totem is the official movie player of the GNOME desktop
environment based on xine-lib or GStreamer (gstreamer is the
default which installs with the arch totem package). It features a
playlist, a full-screen mode, seek and volume controls, as well as
keyboard navigation. It comes with added functionality such as:

- Video thumbnailer for the file manager
- Nautilus properties tab
- Epiphany / Mozilla (Firefox) plugin to view movies inside
  your browser
- Webcam utility (in development)

Totem-xine is still the better choice if you want to watch DVDs.

Totem is part of the gnome-extra group; the Totem webbrowser
plugin is not.

To install separately:

```
pacman -S totem
```

To install the Totem webbrowser plugin:

Useful Applications

```
pacman -S totem-plugin
```

Kaffeine

Kaffeine is a good option for KDE users. To install it, simply type the code below.

```
pacman -S kaffeine
```

Audio Player

Amarok

Amarok is one of the best audio players and music library systems available for KDE. To install it, simply type the code below.

```
pacman -S amarok
```

Exaile

Exaile is a music player written in Python that makes use of the GTK+ toolkit. It tries to be close to the popular Amarok, but in GTK. It is in [community], so install with:

```
pacman -S exaile
```

Rhythmbox

Rhythmbox is an integrated music management application, originally inspired by Apple's iTunes. It is free software, designed to work well under the GNOME Desktop, and based on the powerful GStreamer media framework.

Arch Linux Handbook

Rhythmbox has a number of features, including:

- Easy-to-use music browser
- Searching and sorting
- Comprehensive audio format support through GStreamer
- Internet radio support
- Playlists

To install rhythmbox:

```
pacman -S rhythmbox
```

Quod Libet

Quod Libet is a music manager that uses the GStreamer media framework to play audio files. This allows it to play all the file-types that Rhythmbox (which uses GStreamer too) can play. Quod Libet is more suited to non-Gnome desktops since it has a smaller footprint and fewer dependencies than Rhythmbox (Rhythmbox depends on nautilus, which requires a lot of GNOME to be installed).

In addition to the music player/manager, Quod Libet also includes Ex Falso, a tag editor.

Quod Libet's features include:

- Easy-to-use music browser
- Searching
- Comprehensive audio format support through GStreamer
- Easy Playlist management

To install Quod Libet:

```
pacman -S quodlibet
```

Other good audio players are Banshee and Listen. See Gnomefiles to compare them.

Useful Applications

Moc is a ncurses-based audio player for the console. Other excellent choices are mpd, cmus, and herrie.

Codecs and other multimedia content types (i686 only)

DVD

You can use xine-ui, totem-xine, mplayer or kaffeine (just to name three of the big ones) to watch DVDs. The only thing you may miss is libdvdcss. Beware that using it may be illegal in some countries.

Flash

Install the flash plugin using

```
pacman -S flashplugin
```

to enable Macromedia (now Adobe) Flash in your browser, if you run KDE you should see this after installing flash.

Quicktime

Quicktime codecs are contained in the codecs package. Just type

```
pacman -S codecs
```

to install them.

Realplayer

The codec for Realplayer 9 is contained in the codecs package. Just type

111

Arch Linux Handbook

```
pacman -S codecs
```

to install them. Realplayer 10 is available as a binary package for Linux. You can get it from AUR here.

CD and DVD Burning

K3b

K3b (from **KDE Burn Baby Burn**) is a free software CD and DVD authoring application for GNU/Linux and other UNIX-like operating systems designed for KDE. As is the case with most KDE applications, K3b is written in the C++ programming language and uses the Qt GUI toolkit. K3b provides a graphical user interface to perform most CD/DVD burning tasks like creating an Audio CD from a set of audio files or copying a CD/DVD, as well as more advanced tasks such as burning eMoviX CD/DVDs. It can also perform direct disc-to-disc copies. The program has many default settings which can be customized by more experienced users. The actual disc recording in K3b is done by the command line utilities cdrecord or wodim, cdrdao, and growisofs. As of version 1.0, K3b features a built-in DVD ripper.- licensed under the GPL.

K3b was voted LinuxQuestions.org's Multimedia Utility of the Year (2006) by the majority (70%) of voters.

To install:

```
pacman -S k3b
```

Brasero

Brasero is an application that burns CDs/DVDs for the GNOME Desktop. It is designed to be as simple as possible and has some

112

Useful Applications

unique features to enable users to create their discs easily and
quickly.

To install:

```
pacman -S brasero
```

Abcde is a console-based application for ripping CDs. It supports
encoding immediately after ripping, CDDB, and writing tags on-
the-fly.

Bashburn is a console-based application for burning isos, CDs, and
DVDs. It supports many, if not all of the same things as Brasero and
K3b.

Most CD burners are wrappers for cdrecord:

```
pacman -S cdrkit
```

If you install packages for CD/DVD burning applications like
Brasero or K3B it also installs the CD/DVD burning library for it,
like libburn or cdrkit.

A good command-line DVD-burning tool is growisofs:

```
pacman -S dvd+rw-tools
```

Networking

A good network manager for Linux is wicd. It has few
dependencies (compared to network-manager), is fast and
lightweight and makes a great tool for any laptop or desktop using
wireless networks.

113

Arch Linux Handbook

TV-Cards

There are several things to do if you want to watch TV under (Arch) Linux. The most important task is to find out which chip your tuner is using. However, quite a lot are supported. Be sure to check at a Hardware Database to be sure (see this list, for example). Once you know your Model, there are just a few steps ahead to get you going.

In most cases, you will need to use the bttv-drivers (other drivers exist, like V4L) together with the I2C-modules. Configuring those is the hardest task. If you are lucky, a

```
modprobe bttv
```

will autodetect the card (check dmesg for results). In that case, you need only to install an application to watch TV. We will look at that later, though. If the autodetection did not work, you will need to check the file CARDLIST, which is included in the tarball of bttv to find out the right parameters for your card. A PV951 without radio support would need this line:

```
modprobe bttv card=42 radio=0
```

Some cards need the following line to produce sound:

```
modprobe tvaudio
```

However, that varies. So just try it out. Some other cards demand the following line:

```
modprobe tuner
```

This is subject to trial-and-error, too.

To actually watch TV, install the tvtime-package with

114

Useful Applications

```
pacman -S tvtime
```

and read its manpage.

Digital Cameras

Most **newer** digital cameras are supported as USB mass storage devices, which means that you can simply plug it in and copy the images as you would with external hard drives, or USB sticks.

Older cameras may use the PTP (Picture Transfer Protocol) which requires a "special driver". **gPhoto2** provides this driver and allows a shell-based transfer of the images. Several Graphical Interfaces are available for use with gPhoto2:

- digikam (KDE)
- gthumb (GNOME)
- gtkam (GNOME)

Installation:

```
pacman -S gphoto2
```

USB Memory Sticks / Hard Disks

USB Memory Sticks and hard disks are supported out of the box with the USB mass storage device driver and will appear as a new SCSI device (/dev/sdX). If you are using KDE or GNOME you should use dbus and hal (add them to your daemons in /etc/rc.conf), and they will be automatically mounted. If you use a different Desktop Environment you may have a look at ivman.

115

An Introduction to ABS

ABS is the Arch Linux Build System. It is a ports-like system for compiling sources into installable packages.

'Ports' is a system used by *BSD, which uses simple build scripts residing in a directory tree on the local machine. Each port is simply a directory, named for the installable 3rd party software, and containing a build script. Typically, a *BSD user who wanted to build and install *firefox*, would cd into the corresponding firefox port residing under /usr/ports and do make install clean. The *firefox* sourcecode would then be downloaded from a 3rd party source. According to the port build script, the sources would then be compiled, patched (if directed), and finally, installed to the system.

ABS offers the same functionality by providing build scripts called PKGBUILDs, which contain all information for a given piece of software; The md5sums, source URL, version, license and compilation instructions. In addition, ABS provides the advantage of compiling the sources *into an installable package* with the extension *.pkg.tar.gz*. Obviously, it is a simple g-zipped tarball, but it is cleanly installable/removable/trackable via pacman.

Install the abs package:

```
# pacman -Sy abs
```

After installing the *abs* package with pacman, run the /usr/bin/abs script as root:

```
# abs
```

The *ABS tree* is then extracted under /var/abs, organized according to the installable software.

To build a package from source, create a build directory and copy the abs directory for a given application to the build directory:

117

Arch Linux Handbook

```
$ mkdir ~/abs
$ cp -r /var/abs/extra/slim ~/abs
```

This will move the slim subdir and PKGBUILD script for slim to the build directory.

> **Note:** In addition to PKGBUILDs, some software requires an additional *.install file. See the **ABS** and **makepkg** wiki entries for more information

navigate to the slim build directory and, after modifying the PKGBUILD if desired or necessary, invoke the abs **/usr/bin/makepkg** tool

```
$ makepkg -cs
```

- **-c** Cleans up any leftover files from the source compilation
- **-s** Downloads and installs any missing dependencies by invoking pacman

Install with pacman's -U (upgrade) switch:

```
# pacman -U slim-<version>.pkg.tar.gz
```

Done. Slim sources are downloaded, compiled, compressed into a package and finally, installed.

> **Note:** You may build, clean, install any needed dependencies and finally install the package with one command: **makepkg -csi**. The above example used pacman -U to install as a separate step for informational purposes. See the **makepkg(8)** man page.

Q: Why would I need ABS to compile and create an installable package from source, when I have access to all of the same software via pacman and the binary repos?

118

An Introduction to ABS

A: A few reasons:

- For installing newer, unstable, custom, or development versions of an application.

PKGBUILDs are transparent and simple. Edit the software version and the md5sums of the desired versions within the PKGBUILD, and build and install your custom packages.

- For patching.

Copy the corresponding PKGBUILD to a build directory along with your patch, edit the PKGBUILD, and build/install with `/usr/bin/makepkg`.

- For creating your own packages for yourself, or to share with the community on the AUR.

You are not limited to the PKGBUILDs under /var/abs. Create your own to build from 3rd party sourcecode. They are simple, open and transparent. Explore the prototype PKGBUILD provided at /usr/share/pacman/PKGBUILD.proto

- ABS provides an expedient method for recompiling, if necessary.

For example, to recompile your video or wireless drivers.

- To build an installable package with custom configurations

Enable or disable options in any package by modifying the PKGBUILD

- To build an installable package, further optimized for your machine's architecture,

Specify your CFLAGS in /etc/makepkg.conf.

- To rebuild your entire system, BSD-style, further optimized for your machine's architecure.

Use the makeworld script, or the community-contributed pacbuilder

119

An Introduction to The AUR

The **A**rch **U**ser **R**epository

The ABS tree provides the ability to build all Arch software available in the [core], [extra], [community], and [testing] repositories by providing build scripts on the local machine. In contrast, the AUR does not provide a tree on the local machine, but rather, an unsupported repository of build scripts, sporting a handsome web interface at http://aur.archlinux.org/index.php Also, there is an AUR link tab at the top right of every page on the Arch site.

Once you have navigated to the AUR web page, click on the **Packages** button on the top right. You will be brought to the packages search page.

The general procedure will be:

1. Enter the search criteria into the **keywords** field and click on **go**. The next screen will present all related results.
2. Take note of the **Location** on the package listing. If the package location is in **community**, you have not done your homework, and should simply use pacman or ABS to install. If the location is **unsupported**, continue.
3. Click on the name of the package on the package listing. You will be brought to the Package Details page.

An example for the **yaourt** package:

Arch Linux Handbook

```
yaourt 0.9-2
http://www.archlinux.fr/yaourt-en/
A Pacman frontend with more features and AUR support
unsupported :: system
Maintainer: wain
Votes: 943
License: GPL
Last Updated: Sat, 15 Mar 2008 17:15:20 +0000
First Submitted: Tue, 04 Jul 2006 20:37:58 +0000
Tarball :: Files :: PKGBUILD
```

Click on the **Tarball** link in the last line of the details, and save to a build directory.

Navigate to, and extract the tarball:

```
$ tar -xvf yaourt.tar.gz
```

Enter the build directory and invoke makepkg, which will download the sources, compile, and compress the installation into an installable .pkg.tar.gz package:

```
$ makepkg -cs
```

- **-c** Cleans up any leftover files from the source compilation
- **-s** Downloads and installs any missing dependencies by invoking pacman

Install with pacman's **-U** (upgrade) switch:

```
# pacman -U yaourt<version>.pkg.tar.gz
```

Done.

See the AUR wiki entry for more information.

An Introduction to The AUR

Install an AUR Helper

AUR Helpers like Yaourt and aurbuild add seamless access to the AUR. They vary in their features, but can ease in searching, fetching, building, and installing from over 9000 PKGBUILDs found in AUR.

File and directory explanation

"Shareable" files are defined as those that can be stored on one host and used on others. "Unshareable" files are those that are not shareable. For example, the files in user home directories are shareable whereas device lock files are not. "Static" files include binaries, libraries, documentation files and other files that do not change without system administrator intervention. "Variable" files are defined as files that are not static.

/ (root) The root filesystem, represented by the slash symbol by itself, is the primary filesystem from which all other filesystems stem; the top of the hierarchy. All files and directories appear under the root directory "/", even if they are stored on different physical devices. The contents of the root filesystem must be adequate to boot, restore, recover, and/or repair the system.

/bin/ Essential command binaries that must be available in single user mode; for all users (e.g., cat, ls, cp). /bin/ provides programs that must be available even if only the partition containing / is mounted. This situation may arise should one need to repair other partitions but have no access to shared directories (i.e. you are in single user mode and therefore have no network access). Unlike /sbin, the /bin directory contains several useful commands that are of use to both the root user as well as non-root users.

/boot/ Unshareable, static directory containing the kernel and ramdisk images as well as the bootloader configuration file, and bootloader stages. /boot also stores data that is used before the kernel begins executing userspace programs. This may include saved master boot sectors and sector map files.

/dev/ Essential device nodes created by udev during the boot process and as machine hardware is discovered by events. This directory highlights one important aspect of the UNIX filesystem - everything is a file or a directory. Exploring this directory will reveal many files, each representing a hardware component of the system. The majority of devices are either block or character devices; however other types of devices exist and can be created. In general, 'block devices' are devices that store or hold data, whereas

Arch Linux Handbook

'character devices' can be thought of as devices that transmit or transfer data. For example, hard disk drives and optical drives are categorized as block devices while serial ports, mice and USB ports are all character devices.

/etc/ Host-specific, unshareable global configuration files shall be placed in the /etc directory. If more than one configuration file is required for an application, it is customary to use a subdirectory in order to keep the /etc/ area as clean as possible. It is considered good practice to make frequent backups of this directory as it contains all system related configuration files.

> **/etc/conf.d/** Some daemon scripts will have a matching configuration file in this directory that contains some useful default values. When a daemon is started, it will first source the settings from its config file within this directory, and then source /etc/rc.conf. Arch's simple, transparent scripting approach means you can easily centralize all your daemon configuration options in your /etc/rc.conf simply by setting an appropriate variable value, or, split up your configuration over multiple files if you prefer a decentralized approach to this issue.
>
> **/etc/rc.d/** All Arch daemons reside here. Custom scripts may also be placed here and invoked from the DAEMONS= array in /etc/rc.conf
>
> **/etc/X11/** Configuration files for the X Window System
>
>> **/etc/X11/xinit/** xinit configuration files. 'xinit' is a configuration method of starting up an X session that is designed to be used as part of a script.
>>
>> **/etc/X11/xinit/xinitrc** Global xinitrc file, used by all X sessions started by xinit (startx). Its usage is of course overridden by a .xinitrc file located in the home directory of a user.

126

File and directory explanation

/home/ UNIX is a multi-user environment. Therefore, each user is also assigned a specific directory that is accessible only to them and to the root user. These are the user home directories, which can be found under '/home/$USER' (~/). Within their home directory, a user can write files, delete them, install programs, etc. Users' home directories contain their data and personal configuration files, the so-called 'dot files' (their name is preceded by a dot), which are 'hidden'. To view dotfiles, enable the appropriate option in your file manager or run ls with the -a switch. If there is a conflict between personal and system wide configuration files, the settings in the personal file will prevail. Dotfiles most likely to be altered by the end user include .xinitrc and .bashrc files. The configuration files for xinit and Bash respectively. They allow the user the ability to change the window manager to be started upon login and also aliases, user-specified commands and environment variables respectively. When a user is created, their dotfiles shall be taken from the /etc/skel directory where system sample files reside. **/home** can become quite large as it is typically used for storing downloads, compiling, installing and running programs, mail, collections of multimedia files etc.

/lib/ Contains kernel modules and essential shared library images (the C programming code library) needed to boot the system and run the commands under /bin/ and /sbin/. Libraries are collections of frequently used program routines and are readily identifiable through their filename extension of *.so. They are essential for basic system functionality. Kernel modules (drivers) are in the subdirectory /lib/modules/<kernel-version>.

/lost+found UNIX-like operating systems must execute a proper shutdown sequence. At times, a system might crash or a power failure might take the machine down. Either way, at the next boot, a filesystem check using the *fsck* program shall be performed. *Fsck* will go through the system and try to recover any corrupt files that it finds. The result of this recovery operation will be placed in this directory. The files recovered are not likely to be complete or make much sense but there always is a chance that something worthwhile is recovered.

/media/ Mount points for removable media. CDROMs, DVD's, and USB sticks shall have an appropriate mount point under /media/.

Arch Linux Handbook

The motivation for the creation of this directory has been that historically there have been a number of other different places used to mount removeable media such as /cdrom, /mnt or /mnt/cdrom. Placing the mount points for all removable media directly in the root directory would potentially result in a large number of extra directories in /. Although the use of subdirectories in /mnt as a mount point has recently been common, it conflicts with a much older tradition of using /mnt directly as a temporary mount point. Therefore, Arch allocates /media as the mountpoint for removable media. On systems where more than one device exists for mounting a certain type of media, mount directories shall be created by appending a digit to the name of those available above starting with '0', but the unqualified name must also exist.

The "hal" (Hardware Abstraction Layer) daemon mounts removable media to /media as /media/<name_of_removable_filesystem>

/mnt/ This is a generic mount point for temporary filesystems or devices. Mounting is the process of making a filesystem available to the system. After mounting, files will be accessible under the mount-point. Additional mount-points (subdirectories) may be created under /mnt/. There is no limitation to creating a mount-point anywhere on the system, but by convention and for practicality, littering a file system with mount-points should be avoided.

/opt/ Packages and large static files that do not fit cleanly into the above GNU filesystem layout can be placed in /opt. A package placing files in the /opt/ directory creates a directory bearing the same name as the package. This directory in turn holds files that otherwise would be scattered throughout the file system. For example, the acrobat package has Browser, Reader, and Resource directories sitting at the same level as the bin directory. This doesn't fit into a normal GNU filesystem layout, so Arch places all the files in a subdirectory of /opt.

/proc/ /proc is very special in that it is also a virtual filesystem. It is sometimes referred to as the *process information pseudo-file system*. It doesn't contain 'real' files, but rather, runtime system information (e.g. system memory, devices mounted, hardware configuration, etc). For this reason it can be regarded as a control and information center for the kernel. In fact, quite a lot of system utilities are

File and directory explanation

simply calls to files in this directory. For example, 'lsmod' is the same as 'cat /proc/modules' while 'lspci' is a synonym for 'cat /proc/pci'. By altering files located in this directory, kernel parameters may be read/changed (sysctl) while the system is running.

The most distinctive facet about files in this directory is the fact that all of them have a file size of 0, with the exception of **kcore, mounts** and **self**.

/root/ Home directory of the System Administrator, 'root'. This may be somewhat confusing, ('/root under root') but historically, '/' was root's home directory (hence the name of the Administrator account). To keep things tidier, 'root' eventually got his own home directory. Why not in '/home'? Because '/home' is often located on a different partition or even on another system and would thus be inaccessible to 'root' when - for some reason - only '/' is mounted.

/sbin/ UNIX discriminates between 'normal' executables and those used for system maintenance and/or administrative tasks. The latter reside either here or - the less important ones - in /usr/sbin. Programs executed after /usr is known to be mounted (when there are no problems) are generally placed into /usr/sbin. This directory contains binaries that are essential to the working of the system. These include system administration as well as maintenance and hardware configuration programs. grub (the command), fdisk, init, route, ifconfig, etc., all reside here.

/srv/ Site-specific data which is served by the system. The main purpose of specifying this is so that users may find the location of the data files for a particular service, and so that services which require a single tree for readonly data, writable data and scripts (such as cgi scripts) can be reasonably placed. Data of interest to a specific user shall be placed in that user's home directory.

/tmp This directory contains files that are required temporarily. Many programs use this to create lock files and for temporary storage of data. Do not remove files from this directory unless you know exactly what you are doing! Many of these files are important for currently running programs and deleting them may result in a system crash. On most systems, this directory is cleared out at boot

129

Arch Linux Handbook

or at shutdown by the local system. The basis for this was historical precedent and common practice.

/usr/ While root is the primary filesystem, /usr is the secondary hierarchy, for user data, containing the majority of (multi-)user utilities and applications. /usr is shareable, read-only data. This means that /usr shall be shareable between various hosts and must not be written to, except in the case of system administrator intervention (installation, update, upgrade). Any information that is host-specific or varies with time is stored elsewhere.

Aside from /home/, /usr/ usually contains by far the largest share of data on a system. Hence, this is one of the most important directories in the system as it contains all the user binaries, their documentation, libraries, header files, etc. X and its supporting libraries can be found here. User programs like telnet, ftp, etc., are also placed here. In the original UNIX implementations, /usr/ (for *user*), was where the home directories of the system's users were placed (that is to say, /usr/*someone* was then the directory now known as /home/*someone*). Over time, /usr/ has become where userspace programs and data (as opposed to 'kernelspace' programs and data) reside. The name has not changed, but its meaning has narrowed and lengthened from *everything user related* to *user usable programs and data*. As such, the backronym 'User System Resources' was created.

> **/usr/bin/** Non-essential command binaries (not needed in single user mode); for all users. This directory contains the vast majority of binaries (applications) on your system. Executables in this directory vary widely. For instance vi, gcc, and gnome-session reside here.
> **/usr/include/** Header files needed for compiling userspace source code..
> **/usr/lib/** Libraries for the binaries in /usr/bin/ and /usr/sbin/.
> **/usr/sbin/** Non-essential system binaries of use to the system administrator. This is where the network daemons for the system reside, along

File and directory explanation

with other binaries that (generally) only the system administrator has access to, but which are not required for system maintenance and repair. Normally, these directories are never part of normal user's $PATHs, only of root's (PATH is an environment variable that controls the sequence of locations that the system will attempt to look in for commands).

/usr/share/ This directory contains 'shareable', architecture-independent files (docs, icons, fonts etc). Note, however, that '/usr/share' is generally not intended to be shared by different operating systems or by different releases of the same operating system. Any program or package which contains or requires data that don't need to be modified should store these data in '/usr/share/' (or '/usr/local/share/', if manually installed - see below). It is recommended that a subdirectory be used in /usr/share for this purpose.

/usr/src/ The 'linux' sub-directory holds the Linux kernel sources, and header-files.

/usr/local/ Optional tertiary hierarchy for local data. The original idea behind '/usr/local' was to have a separate ('local') '/usr/' directory on every machine besides '/usr/', which might be mounted read-only from somewhere else. It copies the structure of '/usr/'. These days, '/usr/local/' is widely regarded as a good place in which to keep self-compiled or third-party programs. This directory is empty by default in Arch Linux. It may be used for manually compiled software installations if desired. Pacman installs to /usr/, therefore, manually

131

Arch Linux Handbook

compiled/installed software installed to
/usr/local/ may peacefully co-exist with
pacman-tracked system software.

/var/ Variable files, such as logs, spool files, and temporary e-mail
files. On Arch, the ABS tree and pacman cache also reside here.
Why not put the variable and transient data into /usr/? Because there
might be circumstances when /usr/ is mounted as read-only, e.g. if it
is on a CD or on another computer. '/var/' contains variable data, i.e.
files and directories the system must be able to write to during
operation, whereas /usr/ shall only contain static data. Some
directories can be put onto separate partitions or systems, e.g. for
easier backups, due to network topology or security concerns. Other
directories have to be on the root partition, because they are vital for
the boot process. 'Mountable' directories are: '/home', '/mnt', '/tmp',
'/usr' and '/var'. Essential for booting are: '/bin', '/boot', '/dev', '/etc',
'/lib', '/proc' and '/sbin'.

/var/abs/ The ABS tree. A ports-like package
build system hierarchy containing build scripts
within subdirectories corresponding to all
installable Arch software.
/var/cache/pacman/pkg/ The pacman package
cache.
/var/lib/ State information. Persistent data
modified by programs as they run (e.g.
databases, packaging system metadata etc.).
/var/lock/ Unsharable Lock files data. Files
keeping track of resources currently in use.
/var/log/ Log files.
/var/mail/ Shareable directory for users'
mailboxes.
/var/run/ Unshareable data about the running
system since last boot (e.g. currently logged-in
users and running daemons).
/var/spool/ Spool for tasks waiting to be
processed (e.g. print queues and unread mail).

File and directory explanation

/var/spool/mail/ Deprecated location for users' mailboxes.

/var/tmp/ Temporary files to be preserved between reboots.

Arch Boot Process

After the initial POST, the BIOS directs the computer to load a boot sector from the hard drive. Actually, a small program called GRUB stage1 is within this sector. This is a tiny program. Its only function is to load GRUB stage1.5 or stage2 (depending on filesystem type).

GRUB stage1.5/stage2 will present a boot menu with various (customizable) choices of operating systems to boot. The path to the device, partition and filename of the kernel and initial ram filesystem is contained for GRUB in /boot/grub/menu.lst.

After choosing an Arch Linux entry, GRUB loads the Linux kernel. The kernel is the core of an operating system. It functions on a low level (*kernelspace*) interacting between the hardware of the machine, and the programs which use the hardware to run. To make efficient use of the cpu, the kernel uses a scheduler to arbitrate which tasks take priority at any given moment, creating the illusion (to human perception) of many tasks being executed simultaneously.

After the kernel is loaded, it reads from the initramfs. The purpose of the initramfs is to bootstrap the system to the point where it can access the root filesystem. This means it has to load any modules that are required for devices like IDE, SCSI, or SATA drives (or USB/FW, if you are booting off a USB/FW drive). Once the initramfs loads the proper modules, either manually or through udev, it passes control to the kernel and the boot process continues. For this reason, the initrd only needs to contain the modules necessary to access the root filesystem. It does not need to contain every module you would ever want to use. The majority of your everyday modules will be loaded later on by udev, during the init process.

The kernel then looks for the program init which resides at /sbin/init. init relies on glibc, the GNU C library. Libraries are collections of frequently used program routines and are readily identifiable through their filename extension of *.so. They are essential for basic system functionality. This part of the boot process is called *early userspace*.

Arch Linux Handbook

The purpose of `init` is to bring (and keep) the system up into a usable state. It uses the boot scripts to do so. As you may be aware, Arch uses BSD-style boot scripts. `init` reads the file `/etc/inittab`, which tells it what to do. Looking over the `inittab` script, you will find that the first uncommented line defines the default system runlevel, or, 3. The next thing it is told to do is to run an initialization script. The program that executes (or interprets) this script is bash, the same program that gives you a command prompt. In Arch Linux, the main initialization script is `/etc/rc.sysinit`. `/etc/inittab` also defines your virtual consoles, which are 'respawned' by `/sbin/init` if terminated. Lastly, `inittab` defines a login manager, if starting the system at runlevel 5 is desired. By default the login manager is also respawned by `/sbin/init` if terminated.

`/etc/inittab` directs `init` to call the first boot script, `/etc/rc.sysinit`, after which `/etc/rc.multi` will be called (in a normal boot). The last script to run will be `/etc/rc.local`, which is empty by default.

When started in runlevel 1, the single user mode, the script `/etc/rc.single` is run instead of `/etc/rc.multi`. You will not find an endless symlink collection in the /etc/rc?.d/ directories to define the boot sequence for all possible runlevels. In fact, due to this approach Arch only really has three runlevels, if you take starting up X in runlevel 5 into account. The boot scripts are using the variables and definitions found in the `/etc/rc.conf` file and also a set of general functions defined in the `/etc/rc.d/functions` script. If you plan to write your own daemon files, you should consider having a look at this file and existing daemon scripts.

Boot Script Overview

1. /etc/inittab (covered above)
2. /etc/rc.sysinit
3. /etc/rc.single
4. /etc/rc.multi
5. /etc/rc.local
6. /etc/profile

Arch Boot Process

7. /etc/rc.shutdown
8. /etc/rc.local.shutdown
9. /etc/rc.d/*

/etc/rc.sysinit

The main system boot script, which mounts filesystems, runs udev, activates swap, loads modules, sets localization parameters, etc. When called, udev shall probe system hardware, loading appropriate kernel modules and creating device nodes under /dev. For more, open /etc/rc.sysinit in your editor of choice; the file is well commented.

/etc/rc.single

Single-user startup. Not used in a normal boot-up. If the system is started in single-user mode, for example with the kernel parameter 1 before booting or during normal multi-user operation with the command init 1, this script makes sure no daemons are running except for the bare minimum; syslog-ng and udev. The single-user mode is useful if you need to make any changes to the system while making sure that no remote user can do anything that might cause data loss or damage. For desktop users, this mode is usually quite useless.

/etc/rc.multi

Multi-user startup script. It starts all daemons (such as a logger, a network script, etc) specified in the DAEMONS= array in /etc/rc.conf, after which it calls /etc/rc.local.

/etc/rc.local

Local multi-user startup script. Empty by default. It is a good place to put any last-minute commands you want the system to run at the very end of the boot process. Most common system configuration tasks, like loading modules, changing the console font or setting up devices, usually have a dedicated place where they belong. To avoid confusion, you should make sure that whatever you intend to add to your rc.local is not already residing in /etc/profile.d/, or any other existing configuration location instead.

137

Arch Linux Handbook

/etc/profile This script is run on each user login to initialize the system. It globally defines PS1, $PATH, bash aliases, etc. It is kept quite simple under Arch Linux, as most things are. You may wish to edit or customize it to suit your needs.

/etc/rc.shutdown

System shutdown script. It stops daemons, unmounts filesystems, deactivates the swap, etc.

/etc/rc.local.shutdown (Optional)

Analogous to the /etc/rc.local file, this file may contain any commands you want to run right before the common rc.shutdown is executed. Please note that this file does not exist by default, and for it to work properly, it must be set as executable.

/etc/rc.d/*

This directory contains the daemon scripts referred to from the rc.conf's DAEMONS= array. In addition to being called on boot, you can use these scripts when the system is running to manage the services of your system. For example the command

```
/etc/rc.d/postfix stop
```

will stop the postfix daemon. This directory is not in the $PATH by default, but may be added for convenience. Obviously a corresponding daemon script only exists when the appropriate package has been installed (in this case postfix). With a base system install, there are few scripts in here, but rest assured that all relevant daemon scripts end up here. If you wish, you can, of course, create your own scripts and place them here, to be called by the DAEMONS= array in /etc/rc.conf on system startup.

This directory is pretty much the equivalent to the /etc/rc3.d/ or /etc/init.d/ directories of other distributions, but without all the symlink hassle. The lack of symlink requirement is a defining difference of a *BSD-style init framework, vs a sysvinit.

138

Arch Boot Process

agetty and login

After the Arch boot scripts are completed, the `agetty` program prompts you for a login name. After a login name is received, `agetty` calls `login` to prompt for the login password.

Finally, with a successful login, the `login` program starts your default shell. The default shell and environment variables may be globally defined within /etc/profile. All variables within a users home directory shall take precedence over those globally defined under /etc. For instance, if 2 conflicting variables are specified within /etc/profile and ~/.bashrc, the one dictated by ~/.bashrc shall prevail.

139

Maintaining the system

su

su or **su** - ?

The default behavior of

su

is to remain within the current directory and to maintain the environmental variables of the original user (rather than switch to those of the new user). It sometimes can be advantageous for a system administrator to use the shell account of an ordinary user rather than its own. In particular, occasionally the most efficient way to solve a user's problem is to log into that user's account in order to reproduce or debug the problem.

However, in many situations it is not desirable, or it can even be dangerous, for the root user to be operating from an ordinary user's shell account and with that account's environmental variables rather than from its own. While inadvertently using an ordinary user's shell account, root could install a program or make other changes to the system that would not have the same result as if they were made while using the root account. For instance, a program could be installed that could give the ordinary user power to accidentally damage the system or gain unauthorized access to certain data.

Thus, it is advisable that administrative users, as well as any other users that are authorized to use su (of which there should be very few, if any), acquire the habit of always following the su command with a space and then a hyphen. (login shell option) The hyphen has two effects: (1) it switches from the current directory to the home directory of the new user (e.g., to /root in the case of the root user) by *logging in* as that user, and (2) it changes the environmental variables to those of the new user as dictated by their ~/.bashrc. That is, if the first argument to su is a hyphen, the current directory and environment will be changed to what would be expected if the

141

Arch Linux Handbook

new user had actually logged on to a new session (rather than just taking over an existing session).

Thus, administrators should generally use su as follows:

```
$ su -
```

An identical result is produced by adding the username root, i.e.,

```
$ su - root
```

Likewise, the same can be done for any other user, e.g., for a user named archie:

```
# su - archie
```

Pacman

Pacman is both a binary and source package manager which is able to download, install, and upgrade packages from both remote and local repositories with full dependency handling, and has easy-to-understand tools for crafting your own packages too.

A more-detailed description of Pacman can be found in its article.

Useful commands

To view the options available for a particular operational command, say -**Q**, just append it with -**h**:

```
pacman -Qh
```

To synchronize and update the local packages database with the remote repositories (it is a good idea to do this before installing and upgrading packages):

142

Maintaining the system

```
pacman -Sy
```

To **upgrade** all packages on the system:

```
pacman -Su
```

To sync, update, and **upgrade** all the packages on the system with one command:

```
pacman -Syu
```

To install or upgrade a single package or list of packages (including dependencies):

```
pacman -S packageA packageB
```

You can also sync, update the package database, and install packages in one command:

```
pacman -Sy packageA packageB
```

To remove a single package, leaving all of its dependencies installed:

```
pacman -R package
```

To remove a package and all of the package's dependencies which are not used by any other installed package:

```
pacman -Rs package
```

(**-Rs** is typically preferred vs **R** to remove any package as it will clean up all unused dependencies)

Arch Linux Handbook

To remove all of the package's now unneeded dependencies and also instruct pacman to ignore file backup designations. (Normally, when a file is removed from the system the database is checked to see if the file should be renamed with a ".pacsave" extension.):

```
pacman -Rsn package
```

To search the remote (repo) package database for a list of packages matching a given keyword:

```
pacman -Ss keyword
```

List all available packages in a given repo. e.g., core:

```
pacman -Sl core
```

To list all packages on your system

```
pacman -Q
```

To list all packages on your system without the version strings, we add the -**q** option:

```
pacman -Qq
```

To search (query) the local (your machine) package database for a given package:

```
pacman -Q package
```

To search (query) the local (your machine) package database for a given package and list all pertinent information:

144

Maintaining the system

```
pacman -Qi package
```

To list all files installed by a given *package*:

```
pacman -Ql package
```

Conversely, to find the package that owns a given file (in this example, the *ls* executable):

```
pacman -Qo /bin/ls
```

List all unused packages no longer required as dependencies, (orphans):

```
pacman -Qdt
```

Remove all orphans: (Recommended for experienced users only.)

```
pacman -Rsn $(pacman -Qdtq)
```

Missing libraries: Suppose you receive an error message like this:

```
mplayer: error while loading shared libraries:
libgssapi.so.2: cannot open shared object file: No such
file or directory
```

This may be an indication that a package you have previously installed is now corrupt (some or all of its files are missing). You should try to find the package name that provides the missing shared library. In this example, you could type:

145

Arch Linux Handbook

```
pacman -Ql | grep libgssapi.so.2
```

The first column in the output is the package name:

```
heimdal /usr/lib/libgssapi.so.2
heimdal /usr/lib/libgssapi.so.2.0.0
```

Then, you can just re-install it:

```
pacman -Sy heimdal
```

To defragment pacman's cache database and optimize for speed:

```
pacman-optimize
```

To count how many packages are currently on your system:

```
pacman -Q | wc -l
```

To install a package compiled from source using ABS and makepkg:

```
pacman -U packagename.pkg.tar.gz
```

Note: There are countless additional pacman functions and commands. Try man pacman and consult the pacman wiki entries.

Files

There are a number of files left and created by pacman and other programs to facilitate maintenance and to conform to a safe computing practice. When pacman is installing something, the package contains information on whether to back up a particular

146

Maintaining the system

file. Such files will have the **.pacsave** extension. When you force a
"NoUpgrade" on a file via pacman.conf, it will not be replaced
during an upgrade and the new file will come with the **.pacnew**
extension. For example, you have edited a configuration file
thoroughly and you do not want an upgrade of the respective
package to replace the file with a new one, we must have the
following line in **/etc/pacman.conf**:

```
NoUpgrade = /path/to/config/file
```

To view the differences of the old and new versions of these files,
we can either edit them manually or use a **diff** utility to take note of
the differences. There is an automated tool to find and view such
files available from the **community** repository:

```
pacman -S pacman-contrib
cd ~/
pacdiff # as root
```

There is a bug in the above tool where if you navigate to **/etc** and
run it from there, the paths will be messed up. We remain on the
safer side by being at "home". You may want to run it as user first
in case you happen to be a careless person (you may just overwrite
or remove files because you *think* that is the right way).

There are other types of leftovers depending on the programs
available on your system. Some will create backups with a **.bak**
extension, while others with something like "~" or "-".
Unfortunately, there is currently no way to "automatically" find and
review them. Fear not, as we have no need for automated tools to
deal with such trivial tasks. Simply use **locate** to search for them:

```
locate -e *.~ *.- *.bak
```

And we can use something useful like **vimdiff** to look at the
differences manually:

147

Arch Linux Handbook

```
pacman -S vim
vimdiff file1 file2
```

Tweaks/Finishing touches

Tweaks/Finishing touches

HAL

Since you have now installed a desktop environment/window manager, and if you did not do so earlier, now would be a good time to also install HAL. HAL allows plug-and-play for your mobile phone, your iPod, your external HD's, etc. It will mount the device and make a nice visual icon on your desktop and/or in 'My Computer', allowing you to access the device after you have plugged it in instead of having to manually configure the /etc/fstab file or udev rules for each and every new device.

KDE, GNOME and XFCE all use HAL.

The installation procedure is described in the HAL article. Some information can also be found at Wikipedia.

Backgrounding DAEMONS on startup

To speed up system start up procedure, background selected DAEMONS in /etc/rc.conf by prefixing them with a '@' e.g.:

```
DAEMONS=(syslog-ng @network crond @alsa @hal @fam @kdm)
```

This will enable daemons to load in the background, without waiting for the preceding daemon to load first. In some cases, this may cause issues, especially if you require daemons to start in the specified order.

Prefix any daemons which you do not need with a bang (!) e.g.:

```
DAEMONS=(syslog-ng @network !netfs !crond @alsa @hal
@fam @kdm)
```

(Alternatively, you may also simply remove unneeded daemons from the array).

149

Arch Linux Handbook

Turn off Control Echo in Bash

Some users may have noticed that since the readline update their terminal has been displaying ^C after ctrl+c has been pressed. While this is not a problem, it can be annoying. For any users who wish to disable this, simply add the following to /etc/profile or $HOME/.bash_profile:

```
stty -ctlecho
```

Beautifying Fonts for LCD's

See Fonts

Adjusting Mouse for scroll wheel

While your mouse should be working out of the box, you may want to use your scroll wheel. Add this to your Input Section (mouse0):

```
Option      "ZAxisMapping" "4 5 6 7"
```

Get All Mouse Buttons Working

See Get All Mouse Buttons Working

Configuring Touchpad for Laptops

See Touchpad Synaptics

Adjusting Keyboard Layout

You may want to change your keyboard layout. To do this edit your /etc/X11/xorg.conf and add these lines in the InputDevice Section (Keyboard0) (the example shows a German keyboard layout with no dead keys; alter this to fit your needs).

150

Tweaks/Finishing touches

```
Option        "XkbLayout"    "de"
Option        "XkbVariant"   "nodeadkeys"
```

Additional tweaks for laptops

ACPI support is needed if you want to use some special functions
on your notebook (e.g. sleep, sleep when lid is closed, special
keys...). Install acpid using

```
pacman -S acpid
```

and add it to the daemons in /etc/rc.conf. If you already have **hal**
specified in your DAEMONS, there is no need to add **acpid**. HAL
will automatically detect and load the acpid daemon. Manually, it
can be started by

```
/etc/rc.d/acpid start
```

More-specific information about Arch Linux on various Laptops
can be found at Category:Laptops (English)

Configuring CPU frequency scaling

Modern processors can decrease their frequency and voltage to
reduce heat and power consumption. Less heat leads to a quieter
system; Laptop users will definitely want this, but even a desktop
system will benefit from it. Install cpufrequtils with

```
pacman -S cpufrequtils
```

Edit the config file /etc/conf.d/cpufreq and change

Arch Linux Handbook

```
governor="ondemand"
```

which dynamically increases the CPU frequency if needed (which is a safe choice on desktop systems too). Alter min_freq and max_freq to match your system's CPU spec. If you do not know the frequencies, run *cpufreq-info* after loading one of the frequency scaling modules. You can also comment out or delete the min_freq and max_freq lines: things will work automatically. Add the frequency scaling modules to your /etc/rc.conf modules line. Most modern notebooks and desktops can simply use the *acpi-cpufreq* driver, however other options include the *p4-clockmod, powernow-k6, powernow-k7, powernow-k8, and speedstep-centrino* drivers. Load the module with

```
modprobe <modulname>
```

and start cpufreq with

```
/etc/rc.d/cpufreq start
```

For more details, see Cpufrequtils

Pm-Utils

The pm-utils package will allow you to suspend-to-RAM and hibernate:

```
pacman -S pm-utils
```

Pm-utils wiki page.

Laptop-Mode

The laptop-mode-tools package is sort of a one-stop configuration for all laptop power management utilities. It works in conjunction

152

Tweaks/Finishing touches

with other installed tools to fully configure everything from hard disk spin-down to X display DPMS standby times, if desired.

```
pacman -S laptop-mode-tools
```

Add laptop-mode to your DAEMONS= line in /etc/rc.conf and configure /etc/laptop-mode/laptop-mode.conf.

Add additional repositories

In several special cases, a package may not be in the official repositories for certain reasons, e.g. size or popularity. In these cases, you might find a specialized user repository that maintains the package you want. See Unofficial user repositories for a maintained list of additional repos. Be aware that using the packages you want from AUR might be better in some cases, depending on the type of package you want.

GNU Free Documentation License

GNU Free Documentation License

Version 1.2, November 2002

Copyright (C) 2000,2001,2002 Free Software Foundation, Inc.51 Franklin St, Fifth Floor, Boston, MA 02110-1301 USA Everyone is permitted to copy and distribute verbatim copies of this license document, but changing it is not allowed.

0. PREAMBLE

The purpose of this License is to make a manual, textbook, or other functional and useful document "free" in the sense of freedom: to assure everyone the effective freedom to copy and redistribute it, with or without modifying it, either commercially or noncommercially. Secondarily, this License preserves for the author and publisher a way to get credit for their work, while not being considered responsible for modifications made by others.

This License is a kind of "copyleft", which means that derivative works of the document must themselves be free in the same sense. It complements the GNU General Public License, which is a copyleft license designed for free software.

We have designed this License in order to use it for manuals for free software, because free software needs free documentation: a free program should come with manuals providing the same freedoms that the software does. But this License is not limited to software manuals; it can be used for any textual work, regardless of subject matter or whether it is published as a printed book. We recommend this License principally for works whose purpose is instruction or reference.

1. APPLICABILITY AND DEFINITIONS

This License applies to any manual or other work, in any medium, that contains a notice placed by the copyright holder saying it can be distributed under the terms of this License. Such a notice grants a

Arch Linux Handbook

world-wide, royalty-free license, unlimited in duration, to use that work under the conditions stated herein. The "Document", below, refers to any such manual or work. Any member of the public is a licensee, and is addressed as "you". You accept the license if you copy, modify or distribute the work in a way requiring permission under copyright law.

A "Modified Version" of the Document means any work containing the Document or a portion of it, either copied verbatim, or with modifications and/or translated into another language.

A "Secondary Section" is a named appendix or a front-matter section of the Document that deals exclusively with the relationship of the publishers or authors of the Document to the Document's overall subject (or to related matters) and contains nothing that could fall directly within that overall subject. (Thus, if the Document is in part a textbook of mathematics, a Secondary Section may not explain any mathematics.) The relationship could be a matter of historical connection with the subject or with related matters, or of legal, commercial, philosophical, ethical or political position regarding them.

The "Invariant Sections" are certain Secondary Sections whose titles are designated, as being those of Invariant Sections, in the notice that says that the Document is released under this License. If a section does not fit the above definition of Secondary then it is not allowed to be designated as Invariant. The Document may contain zero Invariant Sections. If the Document does not identify any Invariant Sections then there are none.

The "Cover Texts" are certain short passages of text that are listed, as Front-Cover Texts or Back-Cover Texts, in the notice that says that the Document is released under this License. A Front-Cover Text may be at most 5 words, and a Back-Cover Text may be at most 25 words.

A "Transparent" copy of the Document means a machine-readable copy, represented in a format whose specification is available to the general public, that is suitable for revising the document straightforwardly with generic text editors or (for images composed of pixels) generic paint programs or (for drawings) some widely available drawing editor, and that is suitable for input to text

GNU Free Documentation License

formatters or for automatic translation to a variety of formats suitable for input to text formatters. A copy made in an otherwise Transparent file format whose markup, or absence of markup, has been arranged to thwart or discourage subsequent modification by readers is not Transparent. An image format is not Transparent if used for any substantial amount of text. A copy that is not "Transparent" is called "Opaque".

Examples of suitable formats for Transparent copies include plain ASCII without markup, Texinfo input format, LaTeX input format, SGML or XML using a publicly available DTD, and standard-conforming simple HTML, PostScript or PDF designed for human modification. Examples of transparent image formats include PNG, XCF and JPG. Opaque formats include proprietary formats that can be read and edited only by proprietary word processors, SGML or XML for which the DTD and/or processing tools are not generally available, and the machine-generated HTML, PostScript or PDF produced by some word processors for output purposes only.

The "Title Page" means, for a printed book, the title page itself, plus such following pages as are needed to hold, legibly, the material this License requires to appear in the title page. For works in formats which do not have any title page as such, "Title Page" means the text near the most prominent appearance of the work's title, preceding the beginning of the body of the text.

A section "Entitled XYZ" means a named subunit of the Document whose title either is precisely XYZ or contains XYZ in parentheses following text that translates XYZ in another language. (Here XYZ stands for a specific section name mentioned below, such as "Acknowledgements", "Dedications", "Endorsements", or "History".) To "Preserve the Title" of such a section when you modify the Document means that it remains a section "Entitled XYZ" according to this definition.

The Document may include Warranty Disclaimers next to the notice which states that this License applies to the Document. These Warranty Disclaimers are considered to be included by reference in this License, but only as regards disclaiming warranties: any other implication that these Warranty Disclaimers may have is void and has no effect on the meaning of this License.

Arch Linux Handbook

2. VERBATIM COPYING

You may copy and distribute the Document in any medium, either commercially or noncommercially, provided that this License, the copyright notices, and the license notice saying this License applies to the Document are reproduced in all copies, and that you add no other conditions whatsoever to those of this License. You may not use technical measures to obstruct or control the reading or further copying of the copies you make or distribute. However, you may accept compensation in exchange for copies. If you distribute a large enough number of copies you must also follow the conditions in section 3.

You may also lend copies, under the same conditions stated above, and you may publicly display copies.

3. COPYING IN QUANTITY

If you publish printed copies (or copies in media that commonly have printed covers) of the Document, numbering more than 100, and the Document's license notice requires Cover Texts, you must enclose the copies in covers that carry, clearly and legibly, all these Cover Texts: Front-Cover Texts on the front cover, and Back-Cover Texts on the back cover. Both covers must also clearly and legibly identify you as the publisher of these copies. The front cover must present the full title with all words of the title equally prominent and visible. You may add other material on the covers in addition. Copying with changes limited to the covers, as long as they preserve the title of the Document and satisfy these conditions, can be treated as verbatim copying in other respects.

If the required texts for either cover are too voluminous to fit legibly, you should put the first ones listed (as many as fit reasonably) on the actual cover, and continue the rest onto adjacent pages.

If you publish or distribute Opaque copies of the Document numbering more than 100, you must either include a machine-readable Transparent copy along with each Opaque copy, or state in or with each Opaque copy a computer-network location from which the general network-using public has access to download using public-standard network protocols a complete Transparent copy of

GNU Free Documentation License

the Document, free of added material. If you use the latter option, you must take reasonably prudent steps, when you begin distribution of Opaque copies in quantity, to ensure that this Transparent copy will remain thus accessible at the stated location until at least one year after the last time you distribute an Opaque copy (directly or through your agents or retailers) of that edition to the public.

It is requested, but not required, that you contact the authors of the Document well before redistributing any large number of copies, to give them a chance to provide you with an updated version of the Document.

4. MODIFICATIONS

You may copy and distribute a Modified Version of the Document under the conditions of sections 2 and 3 above, provided that you release the Modified Version under precisely this License, with the Modified Version filling the role of the Document, thus licensing distribution and modification of the Modified Version to whoever possesses a copy of it. In addition, you must do these things in the Modified Version:

- **A.** Use in the Title Page (and on the covers, if any) a title distinct from that of the Document, and from those of previous versions (which should, if there were any, be listed in the History section of the Document). You may use the same title as a previous version if the original publisher of that version gives permission.
- **B.** List on the Title Page, as authors, one or more persons or entities responsible for authorship of the modifications in the Modified Version, together with at least five of the principal authors of the Document (all of its principal authors, if it has fewer than five), unless they release you from this requirement.
- **C.** State on the Title page the name of the publisher of the Modified Version, as the publisher.
- **D.** Preserve all the copyright notices of the Document. .
- **E.** Add an appropriate copyright notice for your modifications adjacent to the other copyright notices.

Arch Linux Handbook

- **F.** Include, immediately after the copyright notices, a license notice giving the public permission to use the Modified Version under the terms of this License, in the form shown in the Addendum below.
- **G.** Preserve in that license notice the full lists of Invariant Sections and required Cover Texts given in the Document's license notice.
- **H.** Include an unaltered copy of this License.
- **I.** Preserve the section Entitled "History", Preserve its Title, and add to it an item stating at least the title, year, new authors, and publisher of the Modified Version as given on the Title Page. If there is no section Entitled "History" in the Document, create one stating the title, year, authors, and publisher of the Document as given on its Title Page, then add an item describing the Modified Version as stated in the previous sentence.
- **J.** Preserve the network location, if any, given in the Document for public access to a Transparent copy of the Document, and likewise the network locations given in the Document for previous versions it was based on. These may be placed in the "History" section. You may omit a network location for a work that was published at least four years before the Document itself, or if the original publisher of the version it refers to gives permission.
- **K.** For any section Entitled "Acknowledgements" or "Dedications", Preserve the Title of the section, and preserve in the section all the substance and tone of each of the contributor acknowledgements and/or dedications given therein.
- **L.** Preserve all the Invariant Sections of the Document, unaltered in their text and in their titles. Section numbers or the equivalent are not considered part of the section titles.
- **M.** Delete any section Entitled "Endorsements". Such a section may not be included in the Modified Version.
- **N.** Do not retitle any existing section to be Entitled "Endorsements" or to conflict in title with any Invariant Section.
- **O.** Preserve any Warranty Disclaimers.

GNU Free Documentation License

If the Modified Version includes new front-matter sections or appendices that qualify as Secondary Sections and contain no material copied from the Document, you may at your option designate some or all of these sections as invariant. To do this, add their titles to the list of Invariant Sections in the Modified Version's license notice. These titles must be distinct from any other section titles.

You may add a section Entitled "Endorsements", provided it contains nothing but endorsements of your Modified Version by various parties--for example, statements of peer review or that the text has been approved by an organization as the authoritative definition of a standard.

You may add a passage of up to five words as a Front-Cover Text, and a passage of up to 25 words as a Back-Cover Text, to the end of the list of Cover Texts in the Modified Version. Only one passage of Front-Cover Text and one of Back-Cover Text may be added by (or through arrangements made by) any one entity. If the Document already includes a cover text for the same cover, previously added by you or by arrangement made by the same entity you are acting on behalf of, you may not add another; but you may replace the old one, on explicit permission from the previous publisher that added the old one.

The author(s) and publisher(s) of the Document do not by this License give permission to use their names for publicity for or to assert or imply endorsement of any Modified Version.

5. COMBINING DOCUMENTS

You may combine the Document with other documents released under this License, under the terms defined in section 4 above for modified versions, provided that you include in the combination all of the Invariant Sections of all of the original documents, unmodified, and list them all as Invariant Sections of your combined work in its license notice, and that you preserve all their Warranty Disclaimers.

The combined work need only contain one copy of this License, and multiple identical Invariant Sections may be replaced with a single copy. If there are multiple Invariant Sections with the same name

161

Arch Linux Handbook

but different contents, make the title of each such section unique by adding at the end of it, in parentheses, the name of the original author or publisher of that section if known, or else a unique number. Make the same adjustment to the section titles in the list of Invariant Sections in the license notice of the combined work.

In the combination, you must combine any sections Entitled "History" in the various original documents, forming one section Entitled "History"; likewise combine any sections Entitled "Acknowledgements", and any sections Entitled "Dedications". You must delete all sections Entitled "Endorsements."

6. COLLECTIONS OF DOCUMENTS

You may make a collection consisting of the Document and other documents released under this License, and replace the individual copies of this License in the various documents with a single copy that is included in the collection, provided that you follow the rules of this License for verbatim copying of each of the documents in all other respects.

You may extract a single document from such a collection, and distribute it individually under this License, provided you insert a copy of this License into the extracted document, and follow this License in all other respects regarding verbatim copying of that document.

7. AGGREGATION WITH INDEPENDENT WORKS

A compilation of the Document or its derivatives with other separate and independent documents or works, in or on a volume of a storage or distribution medium, is called an "aggregate" if the copyright resulting from the compilation is not used to limit the legal rights of the compilation's users beyond what the individual works permit. When the Document is included in an aggregate, this License does not apply to the other works in the aggregate which are not themselves derivative works of the Document.

If the Cover Text requirement of section 3 is applicable to these copies of the Document, then if the Document is less than one half of the entire aggregate, the Document's Cover Texts may be placed on covers that bracket the Document within the aggregate, or the electronic equivalent of covers if the Document is in electronic

GNU Free Documentation License

form. Otherwise they must appear on printed covers that bracket the whole aggregate.

8. TRANSLATION

Translation is considered a kind of modification, so you may distribute translations of the Document under the terms of section 4. Replacing Invariant Sections with translations requires special permission from their copyright holders, but you may include translations of some or all Invariant Sections in addition to the original versions of these Invariant Sections. You may include a translation of this License, and all the license notices in the Document, and any Warranty Disclaimers, provided that you also include the original English version of this License and the original versions of those notices and disclaimers. In case of a disagreement between the translation and the original version of this License or a notice or disclaimer, the original version will prevail.

If a section in the Document is Entitled "Acknowledgements", "Dedications", or "History", the requirement (section 4) to Preserve its Title (section 1) will typically require changing the actual title.

9. TERMINATION

You may not copy, modify, sublicense, or distribute the Document except as expressly provided for under this License. Any other attempt to copy, modify, sublicense or distribute the Document is void, and will automatically terminate your rights under this License. However, parties who have received copies, or rights, from you under this License will not have their licenses terminated so long as such parties remain in full compliance.

10. FUTURE REVISIONS OF THIS LICENSE

The Free Software Foundation may publish new, revised versions of the GNU Free Documentation License from time to time. Such new versions will be similar in spirit to the present version, but may differ in detail to address new problems or concerns. See http://www.gnu.org/copyleft/.

Each version of the License is given a distinguishing version number. If the Document specifies that a particular numbered version of this License "or any later version" applies to it, you have

Arch Linux Handbook

the option of following the terms and conditions either of that
specified version or of any later version that has been published (not
as a draft) by the Free Software Foundation. If the Document does
not specify a version number of this License, you may choose any
version ever published (not as a draft) by the Free Software
Foundation.

How to use this License for your documents

To use this License in a document you have written, include a copy
of the License in the document and put the following copyright and
license notices just after the title page:

```
Copyright (c)  YEAR  YOUR NAME.
Permission is granted to copy, distribute and/or modify
this document under the terms of the GNU Free
Documentation License, Version 1.2 or any later version
published by the Free Software Foundation; with no
Invariant Sections, no Front-Cover Texts, and no Back-
Cover Texts.  A copy of the license is included in the
section entitled "GNU Free Documentation License".
```

If you have Invariant Sections, Front-Cover Texts and Back-Cover
Texts, replace the "with...Texts." line with this:

```
with the Invariant Sections being LIST THEIR TITLES,
with the Front-Cover Texts being LIST, and with the
Back-Cover Texts being LIST.
```

If you have Invariant Sections without Cover Texts, or some other
combination of the three, merge those two alternatives to suit the
situation.

If your document contains nontrivial examples of program code, we
recommend releasing these examples in parallel under your choice
of free software license, such as the GNU General Public License,
to permit their use in free software.

164

LaVergne, TN USA
29 March 2010
177467LV00002B/126/P